Harmonic Anthology

Compiled by
John M. Addey, M.A.

ISBN-10: 0-86690-061-6
ISBN-13: 978-0-86690-061-4

First Printing: 1976
Current Printing: 2012

Cover Design: Jack Cipolla

Published by:
American Federation of Astrologers, Inc.
6535 S. Rural Road
Tempe AZ 85283

www.astrologers.com

Printed in the United States of America

Contents

Preface

This book is intended to serve two purposes. First, it makes readily available a number of important journal articles on harmonics which are otherwise very difficult to obtain. Second, the articles selected for reprinting, arranged as they are in historical order, provide readers with a unique perspective on the evolution and development of the harmonic viewpoint in astrology.

As a publishing event the anthology is significant in two respects. For one thing, it is the first book of its kind—a collection of articles which reveal the actual sequence of ideas and discoveries which have yielded a systematic, scientific approach to astrology. Furthermore, there is significance in the fact that the publication of this book marks the fulfillment of an agreement made by four people in 1971 to publish the "complete package" on harmonics, all the material needed to understand, appreciate and apply the techniques which hold such great promise for the future of astrology. The four of us, John Addey, Charles Harvey, my wife and I are proud—and relieved—to see the job completed. Our original inspiration did sustain us despite a multitude of difficulties, not the least of which has been the 4,000 miles separating the four of us into two pairs over the past three years.

The articles which serve as chapters in this book were selected by John Addey. In most cases John has written a 1976 prefatory remark for the article, but they are otherwise unchanged except for correction of obvious grammatical errors and minor alterations to improve and standardize format. Chapter 15 was specially written by John Addey for this anthology; it serves as an updated version of two earlier articles cited below.

Aside from John's work as compiler, author of 1976 comments and rewriter of the articles combined in chapter 15, he has inserted a few new footnotes which we have not bothered to distinguish from those in the original articles.

Major efforts were expended by two other people besides John. The original articles frequently contained diagrams which were lacking in clarity or precision. As a result all diagrams have been redrawn by the careful pen of Charles Graham. Of equal magnitude was the task of proofing the text, retyping and overall bit-and-piece management. For expertise and dedication in this task I must thank my secretary, Gladys Backmann.

A final remark is in order before giving full citations of articles reprinted in this book. Throughout the time John and others were developing the basic concepts underlying harmonics, a single organization and its people provided a cradle for the brain child and, later on, a home in which it could grow to late adolescence where, I think, the harmonics are today. This organization was of course the Astrological Association of Great Britain. John was its co-founder, president and editor of its journal for many years.

The original articles reprinted in the anthology appeared as follows. Note that the last chapter contains a 1976 revision of two earlier articles.

1. "The Search for a Scientific Starting-Point, Part One," John Addey, *Astrology* XXXII No. 2 (1958).

2. "The Search for a Scientific Starting-Point, Part Two," John Addey, *Astrology* XXXII No. 3 (1958)

3. "The Discovery of the Scientific Starting-Point in Astrology," John Addey, *Astrological Journal* III No. 2 (1961)

4. "The Basis of Astrology, Part One," John Addey and Peter Roberts, *Astrological Journal* VI No. 3 (1964)

5. "The Basis of Astrology, Part Two," John Addey, *Astrological Journal* VI No. 4 (1964)

6. "Astrology and genetics: red hair," John Addey, *Astrological Journal* X No. 3 (1968)

7. "Seven-thousand doctors," John Addey, *Astrological Journal* XI No. 4 (1969)

8. "The Nature and origin of 'degree areas'," John Addey, *Astrological Journal* XII No. 1 (1970)

9. "Harmonics and Hindu Astrology—Part I," Charles Harvey, *Astrological Journal* XII No. 2 (1970)

10. "Fivefold divisions and sub-divisions in astrology," John Addey, *Astrological Journal* XII No. 2 (1970)

11. "The Maps of Delinquents: Comment," John Addey, *SPICA*, Spring 19 70

12. "The Unity of Harmonics, Aspects, Antiscions, Midpoints and Other Mean Points," Axel Harvey, *Astrological Journal* XIV No. 4 (1972)

13. "Michel Gauquelin strikes again, Part I," John Addey, *Astrological Journal* XVI No. 4 (1974). (The *Journal* editor mistakenly identified this issue as XVI No. 3.)

14. "Michel Gauquelin strikes again. Part II," John Addey, *Astrological Journal* XVII No. 1(1975)

15. "Sex of Offspring and Father's Moon Position," John Addey is a revision of two earlier articles, namely, "Sex of Children and the Father's Moon Position," John Addey, *Astrological Journal* XIII No. 4 (1971), and "Sex of Children and the Father's Moon Position—Report of further investigation," Charles Harvey, *Astrological Journal* XIV No. 4 (1972).

Chapter 1

The Search for a
Scientific Starting Point

I am sometimes asked how the understanding of astrology as the harmonics of cosmic periods first occurred to me. This essay tells the story. It was certainly not the result in the first place of abstract theorizing. The now emergent view of astrological realities was forced upon me as a result of the careful study of astrological data and a few sensible deductions patiently followed up.

I had been actively interested in astrology for almost 20 years when, in 1955, I set myself to try to find an acceptable and secure scientific approach to the subject. At that time I had studied the standard textbooks, taken the diploma of the Faculty of Astrological Studies, tried my hand for a year or two at professional work and generally tried to master the main elements of traditional astrology. I never had any doubt about the truth of astrology, but it did not take a genius to see that the received tradition, even in the hands of leading exponents, was in a somewhat battered condition. It was rather like a pictorial masterpiece, handed down from remote times, from which most of the paint had either faded or peeled off, leaving only glimpses of the ancient splendor. Or so it seemed to me.

The first part of this essay has nothing to do with harmonics; it explains rather my early attempts and disappointments and how the first clues were obtained. I started work in the summer of 1955 and the period 1956-57[1] was the period of discovery. By the end of 1957 I had put together this essay which, however, was not published until it appeared in two parts in the summer and autumn issues of astrology in 1958.

During much of this work I had the help of Peter C. Roberts, a fine scientist and mathematician, and without his collaboration progress would have been much more circumscribed.

J.M.A. 1976

* * *

Most of us think of the present century as having marked the beginning of a gradual rebirth or reemergence of astrology. The position today is that some useful advances have been made in various branches of practical horoscopy and that thanks to the work of many astrologers there is now a wide-spread curiosity abroad about our science—a kind of latent interest, widely diffused but as yet unfocused.

Nevertheless, what has been accomplished looks rather small when set against the work waiting to be done. So far as the practical rules of horoscopy are concerned there are a host of uncertainties; the zodiac, the houses, aspects—all present intractable problems which can only be solved by careful, persistent work; the philosophical basis of astrology has yet to be adequately re-expressed in modern times; the metaphysical laws and principles of our subject are uncoordinated; our records are scattered and contain many errors; valuable traditional elements lie buried in the writings of the past which need translating, and new developments and discoveries at home and abroad are neglected for want of those who can follow them up and interpret them to us.

With all this to be done there is a great need for more students. Yet before these can be attracted some of the prejudices against as-

---

[1] With Uranus going over my Ascendant.

trology must be removed so that it may be presented as a serious and worthy study. The chief obstacle is the opposition of the scientific fraternity, and to silence or check their criticism would seem to be the first step to presenting our case to a wider public and so attracting more students.

It was this need to get past the scientists, who stand between us and our future supporters, that has been my motive in undertaking the work here described, and not really any special interest in the scientific side of astrology, still less a desire to attract the scientists themselves whose intervention on a large scale would be more of a hindrance than a help at present. A few sympathetic scientists, yes; but not too many.

One cannot blame the scientists for their opposition; they have their criteria of truth, marvelously sound as far as they go, and our claim that astrology will not fit into the present narrow framework of their thought does not absolve us from demonstrating that even in their own terms astrology can be clearly vindicated.

With these considerations in mind I set out two and a half years ago to find a sound scientific demonstration of the working of astrology. (As others have done too, with varying results.)

The first problem of course was that of obtaining adequate data of some class of people for study, always remembering that reliable times of birth in large numbers are virtually out of the question.[2]

I found that the four published volumes of *Who Was Who* gave dates of birth and death for most of the entries and decided upon a study of longevity. These four volumes (though I had no thoughts of going beyond the latest one when I started) will be referred to frequently hereafter and will be spoken of simply as *Vol. I, Vol. II, Vol. III* and *Vol. IV*. It was Vol. IV, *Who Was Who 1941-50*, on which I started and this yielded 324 men and women

---

[2] Or were in those days.

who had reached or passed their ninetieth year. The noon positions of these were tabulated and I set about combing through them again and again for statistical results which showed an outstanding level of significance.

After a while I asked for help from fellow members of the Astrological Lodge and from readers of *Astrology* in extracting the nonagenarians from the other three volumes of *Who Was Who* and in tabulating the data. I cannot sufficiently thank those who responded so generously; without their help the work would never have been done. It would hardly be right to single out names when so many gave freely of their time and labors; however, there were a few who must have spent countless hours at the task and to them I owe very special thanks.

I must however mention Anthony Kelly of Richmond in whose hands the nonagenarians have been for some time and to whom I am indebted for some of the results which follow.

In all, 970 nonagenarians were collected from the four volumes and they formed the basis of the first study. In describing these first results I must emphasize that only a bare outline is aimed at; free from scientific elaboration, a small fraction of the results only are given and *the intention is to indicate the problems and difficulties of this kind of work and which sort of result seemed most promising and which not.*

Readers will now expect me to tell them perhaps which signs the Sun, Moon and planets occupy most frequently in cases of long life. I too thought it would be as easy as that when I set out.

It will be more to the point if I say frankly that there is no clear evidence that the Sun or Moon in any sign is specially favorable to long life. It may be that certain signs do favor long life, but it is safe to say that one could not demonstrate this from as little as 1,000 cases. (The sidereal zodiac as far as it was studied produced if anything poorer results than the tropical.)

4

In dealing with the planets one is of course up against another of the tremendous (but not insuperable) difficulties which beset the researcher—the irregularities of the planetary motions as seen from Earth. Statistics of sign positions often ignore this point completely. Such statistics are often useless; they not only do not indicate the truth precisely, they sometimes point in the opposite direction. For example, in the case of a fast-moving planet such as Mercury, one might assume that over a decade or so it spends an approximately equal period in each sign. But consider the number of days spent by Mercury in each sign during the decade 1850-59:

♈	♉	♊	♋	♌	♍	♎	♏	♐	♑	♒	♓
262	321	310	234	255	358	348	265	325	362	361	259

A nine- or 12-year period would show rather less variation but then one's cases may in fact come from a 10-year period. If one then presents the results as if Mercury had an equal chance of being in each sign the same number of times, the result would be misleading. Here is a fully worked out example.

Of the 324 cases in *Vol. IV*, 266 were born in the decade 1850-59. This table shows the number of times Mars appeared in each sign with the number of days spent by Mars in each sign during the decade.

	♈	♉	♊	♋	♌	♍	♎	♏	♐	♑	♒	♓
Cases	12	20	18	18	33	42	35	21	19	19	10	19
Days	201	209	292	360	444	460	473	376	252	199	194	194

Making the adjustment to the top line to allow for the inequalities of the bottom, we have:

♈	♉	♊	♋	♌	♍	♎	♏	♐	♑	♒	♓
18	29	19	15	23	27	23	17	23	29	16	29

This shows Mars to be strong in the earthy triplicity but the totals are too low to be conclusive.

In discussing longevity the *Encyclopedia Britannica* emphasizes two points. First, that, of the two sets of factors which promote long life—that is the inherited and the environmental—it is the former which are of overriding importance. (In other words a naturally strong constitution is more important than beneficial conditions in the life.) The second point is that the two things of vital importance in the constitution are the nervous and circulatory systems.

Insomuch as the nervous and circulatory systems represent the communications and transport systems of the body it must be safe to say that the condition of Mercury in the chart has a most important bearing on the length of life.

In connection with this, two things seemed likely to prove outstanding in the statistics. In *Vol. IV* (324 cases) Mercury appeared in positive signs 141 times and negative signs 183 times. This is a good result. It suggested that Mercury in negative signs gave that calmer set of nervous reactions which help to promote long life. It was confirmed in *Vol. III* (285 cases) with Mercury positive 121 times and Mercury negative 161. But such are the disappointments of this work, *Vols. I* and *II* reversed the trend with positive 200 and negative 167.

A similar thing happened with the stations of Mercury. I noticed in *Vol. IV* that a striking number of cases seemed to appear around the days when Mercury was stationary. In *Vol. IV* there were 99 cases born within seven days of a Mercury station as against an expected frequency of 83. (In all statistical results one should of course compare the observed frequency with the expected frequency, i.e. the number which on average would be produced by chance.) *Vol. III* again confirmed this with 91 cases against an expected frequency of 73. However, *Vols. I* and *II* (covering deaths between 1897 and 1928) did not confirm the trend.

I am *firmly convinced* that we are here up against yet another major difficulty in astrological research work of this character.

6

One must always remember that astrology *is the study of effects in the world of flux and change.* A particular rule of natal astrology which applied fifty or a hundred years ago may not apply today. Astrological principles do not change but conditions in time and space do. Today we live in an age of noise and stress; it could well be that the importance for long life of having a calm, sound nervous system (and good arteries) in the mid-twentieth century is far, far greater than was the case before the first Great War.

The way to overcome this difficulty in research, of course, is to avoid having data drawn from too wide a period of time. But in taking the shorter period it becomes even more important to study one's ephemeris for the period chosen so as to allow, in drawing inferences, for the special astronomical peculiarities of the period.

If the sign positions of the Sun and Moon by themselves were inconclusive, the Sun-Moon sign *combinations* were one of the best results. It was outstanding that the sign combinations which occurred most frequently in *Vols. III* and *IV* (609 cases) were combinations of harmonious elements—i.e., fire-air, fire-fire or air-air on the one hand, or the same with water and earth on the other; in other words, positive with positive or negative with negative.

The outstanding sign combinations were as follows:

Vol. IV (expected frequency 4-9)		Vol. III (expected frequency 4-25)	
♏-♋	11 times	♌-♎	11 times
♑-♑	5 times (see below)	♎-♐	10 times
♈-♒	9 times	♉-♓	9 times
♎-♐	9 times	♌-♐	8 times
♎-♒	9 times		
♑-♓	8 times		
♈-♌	8 times		
♍-♐	8 times		

7

(In treating the combinations in this way the Sun and Moon signs were treated as interchangeable—e.g., the 11 cases of Scorpio-Cancer in *Vol. IV* were either of Scorpio Sun with Cancer Moon or Cancer Sun with Scorpio Moon. The five cases of both lights in Capricorn are listed second because if one works it out there is only one chance of both lights in same sign occurring to two of the interchangeable combinations. Thus those five cases are really equivalent to 10.)

It will be noticed that of the twelve outstanding combinations listed only one, Virgo-Sagittarius, was of an "incompatible" combination.

It was most striking that when the lights were transposed to the sidereal zodiac (in *Vol. IV*) the outstanding character of the results was completely lost. Only four combinations scored 8 or more and of these, two were of incompatible combinations!

At the opposite end of the scale, too (the least frequent combinations), the tropical zodiac again showed up more convincingly.

It must be admitted that by singling out just those few combinations which appeared most often one might get a lucky result. A more just and comprehensive way, I suggest, would be as follows. Call those signs which are in trine or sextile, harmonious combinations. Those which are in square, semisextile or quincunx (i.e., incompatible elements), let these be called inharmonious combinations. Both lights in same sign or in opposite signs, let these be called neutral combinations. (One cannot be sure that the one-pointedness of both lights in the same sign would promote long life, and the opposition, though traditionally harmful, does at least strike a balance between compatible elements.)

Thus, to calculate the expected frequency: of the 144 Sun-Moon sign combinations there are 24 neutral, 48 harmonious and 72 inharmonious. The proportion 24:48:72 is the same as 1:2:3. So in *Vol. IV* dividing the 324 cases in the proportion 1:2:3

we should expect 54 neutral, 108 harmonious and 162 inharmonious.

Here are the four volumes (970 cases).

Vol. IV	Observed Frequency	Expected Frequency
Neutral	52	54
Harmonious	127	108
Inharmonious	145	162
Vol. III		
Neutral	34	47
Harmonious	130	95
Inharmonious	130	142
Vols. I and II		
Neutral	65	62
Harmonious	124	122
Inharmonious	178	183

Although the last batch struck a fairly even balance, the overall result is fairly good. *However whether this tendency for the lights to be in harmonious signs is related to longevity or to general success in life, or even to generally agreeable conditions of life—that is a different matter.*

Of the 151 neutral combinations, 72 were of lights in the same sign, 79 lights in opposite signs.

Turning now to aspects, we are again up against the difficulty of planetary motions.

For example, in *Vol. IV* there were 14 conjunctions of the Sun and Mars and 10 oppositions (5° orb). The numbers involved are in any case too small to be significant but disregarding this the expected frequency for each aspect would be, if one did not take into account the relative motions of Sun and Mars, 10 for each aspect.

Thus one might assume that the conjunction was probably helpful to longevity and better than the opposition.

But in the decade 1850-59, from which most of these cases came, the Sun was within a 5° orb of conjunction Mars for a total of just 200 days—but was within the same orb of the opposition for only 30 days. Thus we see Sun conjunct Mars 14 times to be a very "poor" result, and Sun opposition Mars 10 times to be a very "good" one.

This is mentioned only to indicate once more the difficulties of arriving at the astrological truth. Still, if one may be permitted to state the obvious, it is better to arrive at the truth with difficulty than something else easily.

Having calculated the solar aspects for *Vol. IV*, taking all the conventional aspects plus the quintile and keeping inflexibly within defined orbs, I was confronted with the following appalling result.

The expected frequency for each set of solar aspect was 178, and these were the frequencies obtained: Sun-Mars 177; Sun-Jupiter 193; Sun-Saturn 178; Sun-Uranus 168; Sun-Neptune 177; Sun-Pluto 181.

So for these men, who had reached the top of their various professions or fields of activities, whose lives had been crowned by success and recognition and by exceptional length of days—their natal Suns (representing the "life force") *showed no greater than a chance tendency* to gather

vigor and enterprise from Mars, or buoyancy and zest from Jupiter, or diligence from Saturn, or originality from Uranus, or insight and imagination from Neptune, or intensity and penetration from Pluto! *The maps of 324 assorted jellyfish would evidently have done just as well.*

What could the explanation be? The results were not erroneous, they have been completely worked over again, more than once. The obvious explanation is that these men showed an abundance of *good* solar aspects but that this was canceled out by an *absence* of inharmonious contacts. It is true that the trines outnumbered the squares—that at least was a comfort. On the other hand, the squares outnumbered the sextiles by an almost exactly similar number. Thus one could not regard this explanation as very satisfactory. That I was able, as I believe, to find the answer to the mystery, was due to an almost chance decision that whilst I was about the job of classifying aspects it would be no extra trouble to note *if each aspect was applying or separating*. Even so, it was not until other results had mostly proved disappointing that I asked myself what could be the significance, if any, of the fact that there were some 30 per cent more separating aspects than applying.

This question marked the turning point of the researches.

Chapter 2

The Search for a Scientific Starting Point, Part II

It will be seen that so far the work had been of an exploratory nature and had served no more than to reveal a) some of the doubts, difficulties and disappointments liable to surround attempts to find a reliable scientific approach to the problems of astrological research and b) that conventional astrological ideas regarding, for example, the importance of zodiacal signs, aspects and so on, did not for some reason appear to stand up well to close scrutiny.

It was not that there was no truth in them (witness the interesting result as to Sun-Moon sign combinations), but rather that their importance had evidently been exaggerated arid that even the best results were somewhat marginal in their significance and liable to evaporate rather easily when tested further. Perhaps everything needed to be looked at in some new way.

Looking back, my whole approach at this time was perhaps rather naive (although there is plenty of similar work being done today, to similar effect, and sometimes with less honesty about the unsatisfactory nature of the results), but the point which can be seen now to be so significant is that even if I had been fortunate enough to find some really striking results—thank goodness I did not, for I might then have given up research—there would have still been a huge question hanging over everything, a question at that time still barely formulated in the mind: How did it all work?

What was the basis of good results and bad? What were the unifying principles in practice behind the observed effects?

It was the next step which was to prove so crucial in giving the key to these questions.

J.M.A., 1976

* * *

The first part of this article described an attempt to find (from the maps of 970 nonagenarians) a dependable statistical demonstration of the working of astrology. The operative word is *dependable*.

The description given hardly conveys an adequate impression of the trouble taken to find some sort of foothold. All the usual possibilities were explored and a good many others besides. Yet so far as my original purpose was concerned I had to admit that the results at this stage were very disappointing indeed. I had found nothing that I could confidently regard as dependable. No one could have been more surprised, or pained, by this negative discovery than I was. Some of the less striking results may indeed have been better than they seemed but to confirm that supposition would have required a fresh set of data. It was then that I noticed that the solar aspects showed a marked preponderance of separating over applying aspects, and concerning this, after some reflection, I reasoned as follows.

If the preponderance of separating aspects was really significant, it meant that there must be some sort of reaction about the point of the exact aspect. In the cases under consideration, as the Sun drew nearer and nearer to the exact aspect, the astrological effects of the aspect evidently became increasingly inimical to the long-lived temperament. After the point of exactitude had been passed the effects were evidently conducive to long life. Or again, on the day or days prior to an exact solar aspect the number of nonagenarians born must have shown a decline. On the day or days

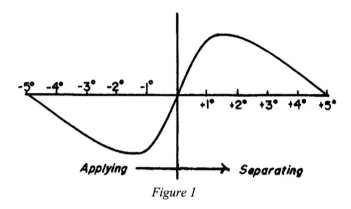

Figure 1

after an aspect the number must have risen suddenly and then gradually returned to about average. Thus if one pictures the Sun moving along in the direction of the arrow in figure 1, applying first by
5° then by 4°, 3°, 2°, 1° and finally reaching the exact aspect, one
can picture the number of cases falling off as represented by the
declining curve. As the Sun moves on to the separating aspect
there is now a sudden rise in the number of cases, the curve swings
upwards—returning to the horizontal line, which of course represents the average (chance)—distribution of cases, as the Sun
passes out of orbs.

Working on this theory I worked through the solar aspects,
once more classifying each aspect according to whether it was applying or separating by one, two, three, four or five degrees. It
seemed to me likely that the more vigorous planets like Mars and
Jupiter might produce a stronger reaction at the point of exactitude
and so I took them first. The result exceeded my best hopes. Here
are the results for the solar aspects to Mars and Jupiter classified as
described. (The average distribution per degree would be 16.)

	Applying						*Separating*				
Degrees	-5	-4	-3	-2	-1	Exact	+1	+2	+3	+4	+5
Mars	15	15	19	18	7	13	25	17	20	18	10
Jupiter	19	18	17	15	9	17	23	25	17	15	18

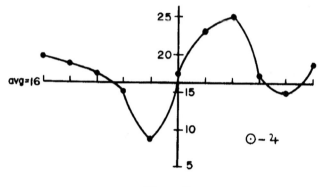

Figure 2

One may set out the Jupiter result, for example, as in figure 2. It is unscientific, I understand, to join up the points as I have done here with a curved line. (This should only be done when it has been proved that there is a gradually increasing and diminishing force in operation and that the points obtained are not just haphazard results). However, the wave-form as shown enables the lay mind to understand more easily what the results imply, i.e. that this could be a true diagrammatic representation of the action of an analogical field of power surrounding the planet.

Figure 3 shows the grand total of all solar aspects to the four "vigorous" planets, Mars, Jupiter, Uranus and Pluto (5° orbs). Saturn and Neptune produced a different curve but then they are of a very different astrological nature. (Venus and Mercury were omitted because of the difficulties of their orbital motion.)

It seemed possible that the (gentle) harmonious aspects might produce a less marked reaction than the (more vigorous) afflictions and conjunctions. The trines, sextiles and quintiles were therefore eliminated from the Mars-Jupiter figures and the quite amazing result is shown in figure 4. Only six cases of the Sun applying by 1° to these planets when the aspect was conjunction, semisextile, semisquare, square, inconjunct, sesquisquare or opposition, but 34 cases of a 1° separation.

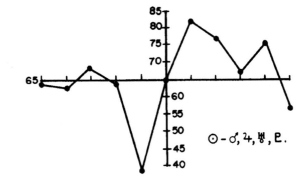

Figure 3

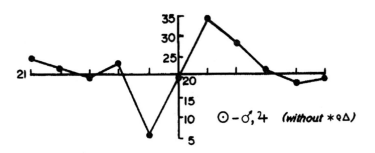

Figure 4

I doubt on theoretical grounds if my first view about the afflictions producing a stronger reaction than the harmonious aspects can be *generally* applicable. It would depend upon what kind of horoscope one was studying presumably.

The most likely hypothesis for explaining these results would run somewhat as follows. The aspects do, as all astrologers believe, bring the planets into a definite relationship with one another. As the two bodies gradually approach the point of the exact aspect a state of growing tension is set up. As the aspect is consummated there is an interchange of power, the tension is discharged and resolved into a state of harmony and balance. In the symbol-

17

ism of astrology the applying aspect thus becomes one of striving, activity, tension and instability. The separating aspect becomes one of tranquility, passivity, stability and inertia.[3]

The symbolism of each kind of aspect is crystallized as it were in the temperament of those born under them, and on this basis it is obvious that the long-lived temperament must be predominantly of the latter type, with a majority of separating aspects.

* * * * *

The best way of testing this theory seemed to be to find a group of people in whom the qualities of the applying aspects (those of striving, activity, tension and instability) might be expected to predominate, and then see if there were in fact a larger number of applying aspects of an *appropriate type* in their horoscopes.

To take those who died before a normal life span was the obvious step, but one does not want to give the impression that astrology is merely concerned with predicting the length of life.

It so happens that I have been concerned professionally for a long time in teaching children who are in hospital with poliomyelitis. Now there are certain recognized characteristics of the polio sufferer. It is considered medically that he tends to be of an exceptionally active, even restless, physical type. It is recognized educationally that the child with polio tends outstandingly to belong to a very active mental type. A dull child is rare in a polio ward, most tend to be of better than average intelligence, though the "butterfly mind," chatterbox type is not uncommon.

All this suggests that those who have a hyperactive nervous system, indicating a high measure of mental and physical activity, are the ones who are most vulnerable to polio.

---

[3] In the light of subsequent studies this hypothesis seems to be an over-simplification.

(Needless to say, "catching" polio is not just a case of having the virus in the system. In an epidemic in Chicago, 78 percent of the population in part of the city were found to have the virus in their bodies, but only one person in 200 was getting paralytic polio.)

This statement by a Dr. Dennis Geffer (quoted from the *Lancet* of October 1, 1955, p. 719) explains the matter further:

"Poliomyelitis is a mild disease with the exception of one complication. This complication is the invasion of the nervous system, the destruction of the nerve cells and the production of paralysis. . . . There seems to be some sort of barrier between the nervous system and the rest of the body which normally is sufficient to prevent the passage of the virus of poliomyelitis. Under certain circumstances the barrier is weakened and breaks down. It may be that local injury, over-fatigue, operations, injections and the like may cause the barrier to break down locally."

What a revealing statement this is to an astrologer; all the things which are mentioned as rendering the nervous system susceptible of invasion are of a Mars character—over-fatigue, operations, injections, local injury. On the other hand the protective barrier (Saturn) is faulty.

From all this, and in the light of our theory, one would look, in polio, for maps in which applying aspects predominate, especially at any rate in the case of Mercury-Mars. Mercury-Saturn might show a low result.

I was able to secure 1,025 dates of birth of polio children—virtually all paralytic.

Once again I must acknowledge the generous help and cooperation of a number of readers of Astrology *in sorting out and tabulating the data of these cases. It was a huge job and again the work would have been impossible without this invaluable assistance.*

In classifying the aspects according to the number of degrees by which they were applying or separating, I decided, with these thousand cases of polio, to include not only the recognized aspects with an orb of 5°, but to include the whole ecliptic—that is so as to include every contact between the two planets under consideration regardless of whether they were near a conventional aspect or not. In this way it would be possible to tell: (a) what happened to the angular relationship between two bodies when they tended not to be in conventional aspect, and (b) if the wave forms which were found near the aspect points extended right round the ecliptic.

This was done, in effect, by classifying the aspect according to the number of degrees by which it was applying or separating from the 12 30°-interval aspects starting from the conjunction (i.e., taking in an orb of 15° at either side of these points).

Figure 5a shows the whole distribution of the aspects between Mars and Mercury *considered as applying or separating from these 12 aspect points*. Figure 5c. shows what happens if the same aspects are considered as applying to or separating from the 24 aspect points at 15° intervals round the ecliptic (i.e., aspects of 15°, 30°, 45°, 60°, etc.) The second result in particular stands out clearly as a triumphant vindication of our theory—the curve obtained is exactly the reverse of the longevity curve which showed a predominance of separating aspects—here it is the aspects applying by 1° which are highest—those which are separating by 1° which are lowest, showing that the very active "polio temperament" correlates with the applying aspect.

Figure 5b shows the distribution of Mercury-Saturn aspects in the same way. Here the striking thing is the way in which the aspects have, as it were, been pushed out from the 30° aspects towards the intermediate 15° aspects. (In fact there are, as one can see, 313 aspects within a 5° orb of the conjunction, semisextile, sextile, square, trine, inconjunct and opposition, as against 424 within the same orb of the aspects of 15°, 45°, 75°, 105°, 135°, and 165°.) The likelihood of such a distribution occurring by chance is

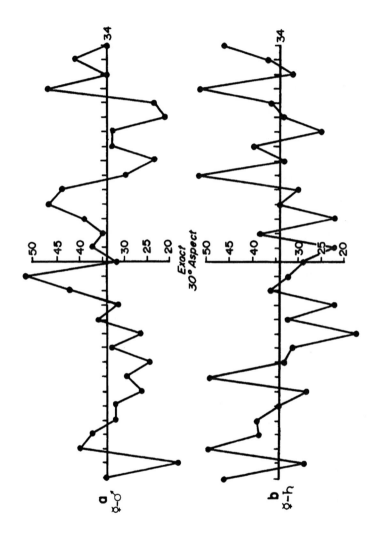

Figure 5
Distribution of Mercury Aspects for Polio Victims

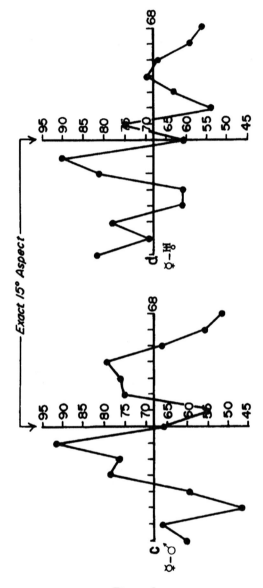

Figure 5
Distribution of Mercury Aspects for Polio Victims

over 500 to 1 against. There is much food for thought here. It quite makes one's heart sink to realize how much more complicated than we assume the whole problem of aspects. may be. Still it is better to know the worst than work in the dark.

One may assume that the 30° interval aspects starting from the conjunction are the dominant series and the lack of these aspects confirms our supposition that the Mercury-Saturn principles would prove to be badly integrated in the polio subjects, shown (a) lack of restraint in nervous activity and (b) failures in the protective barrier round the nerves.

Figure 5d shows the Mercury-Uranus aspects (on the same basis as 5c). These aspects have been associated with paralysis (see *Encyclopedia of Psychological Astrology* by C. E. O. Carter) and here again there are an abundance of closely applying aspects.

It will be seen in figures 5a and 5b that there is a general trend to the line as well as the lesser fluctuations from degree to degree. In the case of Mars there is a big wave in the center and in the case of Saturn a large trough in the center.

Mr. Peter Roberts, who very kindly helped in assessing my results, drew up a diagram of these general trends in a batch of results (not specially selected) which I had given him. This is shown in figure 6. (For those interested, this was obtained by making a 5° moving average of the various sets of results and then striking a line through the points obtained. The scale used emphasizes the curves against figures 5a and 5b.

Mr. Roberts calculates that the average position of the top of the crests in these wave forms obtained empirically, coincides with the exact aspect points to within 0.1 of a degree. A striking proof (for those who need one) of the doctrine of astrological aspects. A comparison of the overall totals of the crests and troughs by the chi-square test shows that the chance of such a distribution occurring in a random selection is of the order of several hundred to one.

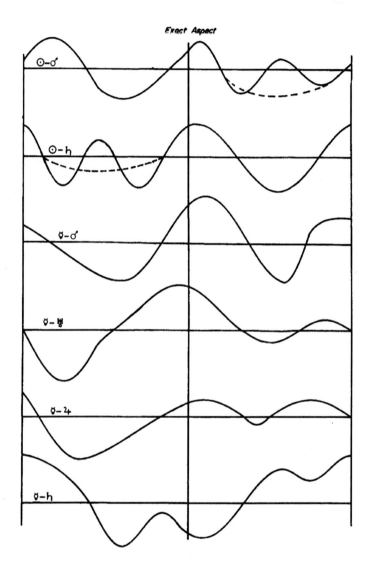

Figure 6
Illustration of General Trend of Aspect Distribution in Polio Cases

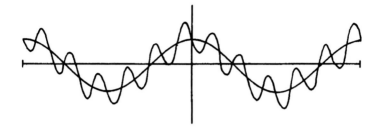

Figure 7

The interpretation of these results, I believe, depends upon a branch of mathematics called wave-form analysis, whereby as I understand it, wave forms, if genuine, can be analyzed into their component harmonics. (Would any reader proficient in this skill care to examine the full results?)

When I began this work I had no knowledge whatsoever of these matters, but it was gradually borne in upon me that the results produced could approximate to a system of superimposed wave-forms as in figure 7. It will be noticed, for instance, in the Mercury-Saturn line (figure 5b) if one starts from the point applying by 10°, then takes the results in pairs moving to the right, the left-hand number is higher than the right-hand one for a 10° orb on each side exactitude.

This appears in other results and suggests an *alternating rhythm of positive and negative degrees.*

To sum up here, as it seems to the writer, are some of the possible fruits of these results if they are confirmed:

To those "outside" astrology and enquiring as to the veracity of our science they demonstrate:

1. That there is a relationship, through the time of birth, between the planetary motions and individual man's bodily nature and by implication with his temperament and destiny.

2. That because the character of the curves differs from one planet to another and because the aspect-points are shown to produce a variation of effects, two of the central tenets of astrology—the Doctrine of Planetary Natures and the Doctrine of Aspects—are true.

To those "inside" astrology and wishing to extend the knowledge of its laws they indicate a technique of determining:

1. The proper orbs to be allowed for each planet and aspect.

2. The positions, effectiveness and relative strength of the different aspects. (For example, what of the quintile and novile series?)

To those practicing astrology and concerned with the interpretation of horoscopes, they suggest:

1. That it may be necessary to draw a distinction between an applying and a separating aspect, considering an aspect between applying bodies to manifest their interaction in a manner more lively, enterprising, progressive and adaptable (or restless, aggressive, volatile and erratic) and those between separating bodies more calm, stable, persistent and conservative (or complacent, inflexible, sluggish and inert).

2. That the strongly effective orb of an aspect may be very small, both for major and minor aspects and alike for lights and planets, the wider orb being regarded as a background influence.

3. That in terms of directional astrology it may be that the formation and separation of a progressed aspect will have to be viewed as having not one point of action, but, say, three, corresponding to the three critical points of the aspect curve—the exact point of the aspect, and the points which seem to occur about one degree before and after. This is less novel than it may seem. Consider the fact that the separating afflictions of Mars were evidently highly beneficial for long life. Is it not our common experience

that a Martian crisis, say a fever, is preceded by a period when impurities accumulate with debilitating effect, and is followed, often by a period of enhanced well-being? Other points will probably have occurred to the reader.

It may have seemed that in parts of this article I was attacking traditional astrological teachings. On the contrary I have confidence in all the matin traditional beliefs. My intention has been to indicate that some may be incomplete as they stand at present, and more particularly that many of them are unsuitable for statistical work because of the thousands of cases which would be needed to reach a conclusion.

May I end by acknowledging again the work of all who have helped indirectly to produce this article and hoping that some way will be found for bringing about better organized collaboration between astrologers in the future?

Chapter 3

The Discovery of the Scientific Starting Point in Astrology

It will be seen that by the end of the last chapter, the seed of an idea had distinctly emerged. But its precise nature and, even more, its implications, had to be thought out, tested and developed.

By the end of 1960, I had been able to consolidate the findings, digest their nature and implications more fully and test the general hypothesis on other data such as the studies by Bradley and Firebrace of birth dates of clergymen.

In my next article, here given, I tried to present the whole picture in a more coherent form. In revising this article, which appeared in the *Astrological Journal* for Spring 1961, for republication, I have left it very largely in its original form but in one or two places where the original was clumsily or inaccurately expressed (due usually to vagueness or uncertainty in my own mind) I have omitted or rewritten such passages lest they should leave a misleading impression in the reader's mind.

Those who are familiar with the mathematics of wave forms will no doubt see in this article the efforts of a beginner to make sense of the subject which was quite unfamiliar to him.

J.M.A., 1976

What largely governs the progress of science—both particular sciences and science in general—is always the ideas at the back of the scientist's mind, the overall picture he has of the problems he is dealing with and the framework of thought in which he sets them. It is for this reason that most scientists of today do not examine astrology; it simply does not fit into their general picture of things. These tacitly accepted concepts determine what the scientist shall look for, what experiments perform, what data accept and what reject. We do this ourselves constantly in our own study of astrology. One can point to endless examples in the history of science of how a wrong overall picture has held up the progress of a science for centuries. The epicycles of Ptolemaic astronomy are an obvious example.

Once the right framework of thought is found, everything falls into place. Even the difficulties which before appeared baffling suddenly become at least intelligible so that their solution is seen to be simply a matter of time. Such changes always involve a fundamental change of viewpoint—a very hard thing to make.

I believe that I have made certain discoveries about the process of astrological cause and effect which, if conceded, must mean that the concepts at the back of our minds have been wrong or inadequate—that in fact we have been looking at things in the wrong way—and that this fact has effectively blocked our progress in every department of our science.

We must begin by considering the ever-changing life of nature and in particular the way in which the ebb and flow of all natural processes can be represented by *wave forms*.

All things that come into the world have their beginnings and endings, appear and disappear; living things are born and die, all have their periods of increase and decrease. *Thus all the processes of nature can be represented in their ebb and flow by wave forms.*

It is this great sea of nature which is the subject of astrology,

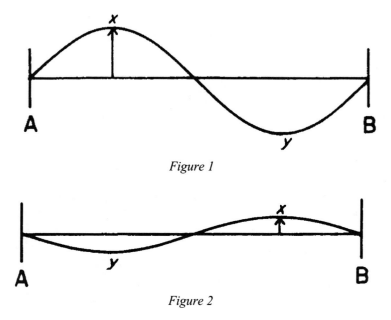

Figure 1

Figure 2

which studies its secondary motions in terms of its primary (celestial) motions. Thus astrological laws can also be considered in terms of waves. Let us have some examples and at the same time *learn three important terms*.

Figure 1 shows one complete wave. One can imagine that it is one in a continuous series of waves. One may think of it in terms of any natural phenomenon—say the rise and fall of the tide. The horizontal line would then represent the level of the sea if there were no tide; point X will be high tide and point Y low tide.

From A to B will represent the time taken for one complete tidal process and this period will be marked off in hours. Let us call AB the FREQUENCY of the wave; this is the period of one complete fluctuation. It will be seen that the amount by which the tide rises and falls is marked by an arrow; let us call this amount the AMPLITUDE of the wave. It will also be seen that high tide comes a quarter of the way along the scale of hours AB; next day, as we know, it will be a little later. Let us call this relationship of the wave to the horizontal scale of measurement the PHASING of the wave.

We can now say that if figure 2 represents the rise and fall of the tide on another day, then the frequency of the tide is the same as in figure 1, the amplitude is now smaller (because not all tides are equally high and low), and the phasing is different (because since each tidal process takes a little over 12 hours, the time of high tide will shift, day by day, in relation to the scale of 24 hours).

But in the world of actuality no one natural rhythm acts entirely on its own. The Moon affects the tides and sets up its own rhythm, so does the Sun, adding a rhythm of its own. Thus these two rhythms mingle together and geographical factors modify them still further. Therefore in nature we are dealing not with simple wave forms but always with wave complexes.

Figure 3a shows two simple waves in the ratio of 1:2, that is to say the length or frequency of the shorter wave is exactly half of the longer one. In such a case one can speak of the longer wave as the first or fundamental harmonic, and the shorter one as the. second harmonic.[4] If the long wave were exactly divided into seven smaller waves, these would represent the seventh harmonic and so on.

Notice that if the second wave is so phased that its crest does not come at the same point as the crest of the main wave, then the result of combining them (figure 3b) is to shift the crest of the combined waves to one side. This is obvious but important.

Musical vibrations provide us with further examples of wave complexes. A tuning fork gives something very near to a simple harmonic, as in figure 1—but other musical instruments give vari-

---

[4] This is not the nomenclature used in music where the basic note is called the fundamental, but the first harmonic is twice the frequency and an octave higher—what we have called the second harmonic.

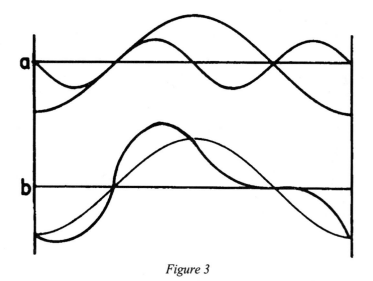

Figure 3

ous vibratory overtones which are harmonics of the main frequency of the note which is being played. It is this which gives to
each instrument its special flavor. Figures 4 and 5 show the sound
waves of a clarinet and oboe organ pipe respectively. (As given in
Groves *Dictionary of Music*.) In both these the "peak" is off-center.

Figure 6 shows heartbeats drawn by an electro-cardiogram.
Here we have all the rhythms of a highly complex cell structure
working together to fulfill the purpose for which the whole organ
exists. Each part of the organ must have a regular rhythm of its
own but together they combine in such a way as to produce those
spasmic contractions which send the blood coursing through the
veins.

Figure 7 shows Helmholtz's curve of dissonance. Helmholtz,
a pioneer in this field, constructed a graph to show the relative
amounts of discord at every point throughout the octave. The line
seems to follow no orderly pattern but it is in effect based on a
complex of regular harmonics.

33

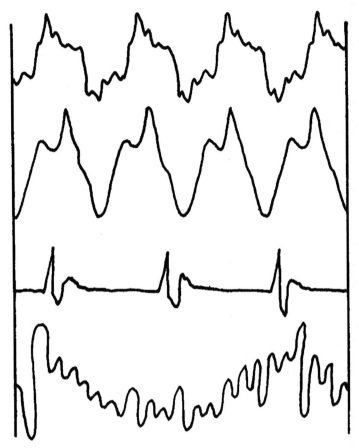

Figures 4, 5, 6, and 7 (top to bottom)

In 1958, I published an article in *Astrology* entitled "The Search for a Scientific Starting-Point." One of the diagrams showed the disposition of Mercury in relation to Mars on the birth dates of 1,024 sufferers from poliomyelitis (see figure 8a). One must imagine that the position of Mars (or an exact 30° aspect point to Mars) is at the center where the two axes cross. The points along the wavy line show the number of times which Mercury was placed so many degrees applying to, or separating from, Mars (or a

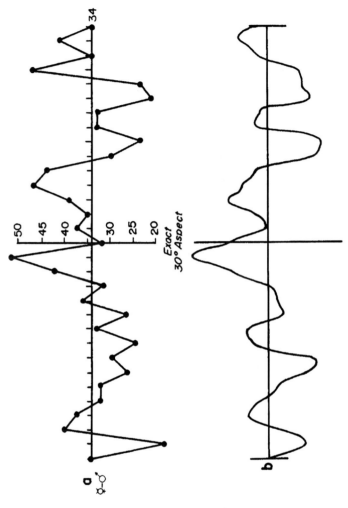

Figure 8

Mars aspect). It will be seen, for example, that the lowest point in the series comes when Mercury is 14° away from a 30° aspect to Mars (there are no more than 20 such positions in 1,024 cases) and that the highest point comes when Mercury is *applying by one degree* to a Mars aspect (there are over 50 such cases).

Now although this Mercury-in-relation-to-Mars distribution pattern may seem something of a puzzle, it is dominated by four harmonics of this 30° period—the 1st harmonic (a wave of 30°), the 2nd (two waves of 15°), the 6th (six waves of 5°) and the 10th (ten waves of 3°). In Figure 8b I have drawn out, with the help of graph paper, the result of combining four such sets of waves and, as will be seen from a comparison of the second (constructed) wave-complex with the original, although it does not exactly re-produce the original, it does account for all its main features.

To put the matter a different way, the relationship of Mercury to Mars could be anything from 0 to 360 degrees—better to regard it thus than 0 to 180)—but if we begin by dividing the circle by 12 (as we have done to get a 30-degree run) it is obvious from figure 8b that the relation of Mercury to Mars in the polio cases is largely governed by the first, second, sixth and tenth harmonics of that series. That is to say, by adding to the 30-degree wave three other wave series whose frequencies are one-half, one-sixth and one-tenth of its length.

In this example the 30-degree wave is phased with its crest approximately on the 30-degree aspect point and has an amplitude of about nine percent. The 15-degree wave is phased with its crests at the 15- and 30-degree intervals and has an amplitude of about 10 percent. The 5-degree and 3-degree wave frequencies are phased so that they both have a crest just before the exact 30-degree aspect point and their amplitudes are about 15 percent and seven percent, respectively.[5]

One result of this phasing is to bring all the waves to a crest (virtually) at one point and one point only—that is, just before the exact 30° aspects—hence the high reading at that point.

In figures 9a and 9b I have taken the 1,024 cases of polio in two groups according to the two hospitals from which the cases

---

[5] This was my first attempt at judging the amplitude of the waves—I should say that the figures given are definitely approximate.

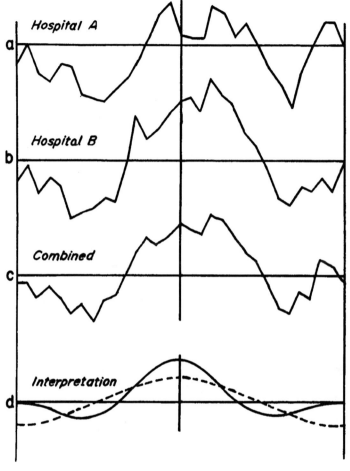

Figure 9

were drawn, and made a 5-degree moving average of both. The effect of this is to smooth out the 5° wave and the 3° wave—but to reveal the two longer waves combined as shown in diagram 9c.[6]

---

[6] In *Astrology* (Autumn, 1958) I give other examples of aspect harmonics in the horoscopes of victims of poliomyelitis and also in the maps of 970 nonagenarians.

Let us now consider a different matter. So far we have been dealing with the relation of one planet to another. What about the relation of a planet to its position in the ecliptic—its zodiacal position as we would usually say.

A few years ago Donald Bradley made a study of sign positions in the birth dates of 2,492 eminent American clergymen, and more recently the Astrological Association has repeated his experiment, using British clergymen. In doing this the Association naturally followed the methods laid down by Bradley. They could not very well have done otherwise if they were to repeat his experiment.

Now I would like to make it clear that although I have never accepted Bradley's conclusions, in favor of the sidereal zodiac, I have always been completely with him in this one essential: that he takes his stand upon the simple proposition that if a thing is true it can be shown to be true. In no other science is it so important to adhere to this principle as in the quicksands of astrology, for in no other science is the scope for self-deception so great.

I know therefore that if I offer a revised interpretation of the Bradley-Association figures on clergymen, that those concerned will take my observation as being all part of the process of sifting for truth which must go on in all scientific work. I offer my views with a keen sense of gratitude and admiration for the work they have done.

Before examining again the main features of Bradley's approach let us carry straight on with our idea of wave forms and see if it is in any way applicable to zodiacal position.

We usually tend to think of the signs of the zodiac as being like 12 sectors or "boxes" placed end to end along the ecliptic. When we move out of one we are immediately in the next one and apart from the fact that we notice that certain degree areas seem to have a curious connection with certain things, we generally regard the "influence" of each sign as being uniform throughout—i.e., once the Sun gets into Aries it has a constant Aries quality until it passes into Taurus. The possible exceptions to this are that some people believe that there is a certain amount of "merging" at the end of one sign and the beginning of the next—and of course the presumed existence of decanate and similar influences.

But suppose we stop thinking about "boxes" and start thinking about waves—what then?

In figure 11, I have taken the Sun's position in each of the zodiacal signs in the maps of the clergymen (all 4,465 of them—2,492 American and 1,973 British)—and added them up so that the first point on the graph is the total number of times the Sun is in the first degree of the 12 signs, the second point represents the total Sun positions in the second degree and so on.

In order to see the general trend of the distribution I have done exactly what I did for the Mars-Mercury aspects in figures 9a, b and c, that is, smooth the distribution by taking a five-degree moving average. Thus figure 10 shows a) five-degree moving average for the Association clergy b) ditto for Bradley, c) both combined and d) the interpretation of the distribution as a combination of two waves as in the Mercury-Mars distribution. This time the totals are much higher, (the mean is 150 cases per degree) and the steadiness of the line therefore reflects the high measure of stability which the results show—thus one can see even more clearly the agreement between the actual totals and the ideal synthesis of the two waves.

Before proceeding we may notice briefly that at any point along a wave whose frequency is 30 degrees or any sub-multiple of that (½ x 30, ¼ x 30, etc.) a 30-degree moving total is taken, then the positive and negative phases of the wave *will always exactly cancel each other out* (figure 12). *Bradley's work was based on 30-degree moving totals, thus his results could never show a 30-degree wave, nor any wave whose frequency exactly divides into 30.*

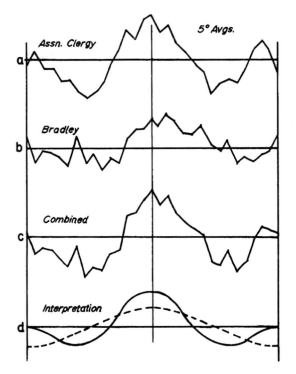

Figure 10

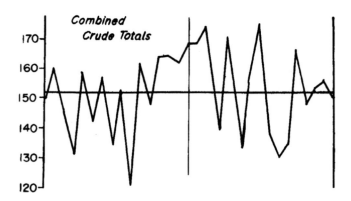

Figure 11

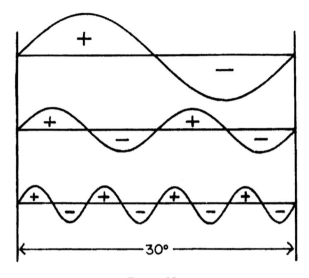

Figure 12

But now the subject suddenly opens out. So far we have examined the 12th harmonic of the ecliptic only—i.e., that frequency which divides the circle into 12 waves with the possible subdivisions thereof. But why only the 12th? We are like musicians trying to play a tune on one note!

It will be seen that the ecliptic could be divided by all the numbers from 1 to 180 and beyond to give 180 possible wave frequencies of two degrees or more in length—though of course most of these frequencies will not be of a whole number of degrees. If we begin by dividing the circle into *12* lengths of 30 degrees each, and regard this length as our fundamental harmonic, we can subdivide it into smaller length's—but each of these must be an exact subdivision of 30 degrees. Thus, again confining ourselves to those frequencies which are two degrees or more in length, we can obtain from this 12th harmonic, 15 possible frequencies. These are: 1 wave of 30 degrees, 2 of 15, 3 of 10, 4 of 7½ and so on down to 15 of 2 degrees. Thus the original division by 12 gives us only 15 of the 180 possible frequencies of two degrees or more.

If we divide the circle by 11 and take its sub-frequencies, we immediately get 15 *new* frequencies as well as that which is 1/132 of the ecliptic and which appeared in the 1/12 series. The division by 10 gives 14 new harmonics; by 9, 13 more; by 8, 10 more; by 7, 15 more and so on till we have used up all the 180 possible frequencies of two degrees or more in the ecliptic.

Upon investigation, it is found that if the Sun's distribution in the clergyman nativities is considered in terms of all the major harmonic series (as described in the previous paragraph) many, if not most, of them show a better than chance distribution despite the fact that each harmonic series is to a large extent self-contained. In some of these series (e.g., the 12th) the odds-against-chance of the distribution are very small, no better than 5:1. But in others the significance is very high, e.g. the seventh which shows a distribution with odds of over 100:1 against chance.

Let us therefore look at the seventh harmonic. Figure 13 shows the Sun's total distribution along successive sectors of the ecliptic each 1/7 of the ecliptic in length and taken together as one series in the Association clergymen *control* experiment (1,973 dates based on random numbers and distributed by years in a similar way to the 1,973 clergymen birth dates).

In this series, in other words, the first total on the left is not the total for the first degree of all 12 signs, but as if for the first degree of a seven-sign zodiac—each sign being of course 51½ degrees in length.

Figure 13a shows the Sun's distribution in the *control*; figure 13b shows the distribution in the *clergymen* nativities. In order to see the striking difference between these one may stand a yard or two away from the diagram; the points on the graph in the *control* are distributed about a straight line—those in the *clergymen* show a general trend which is not a straight line—those in the *control* show only a small tendency to diverge from the mean distribution—those in the *clergy* show a vigorous oscillation. But what is

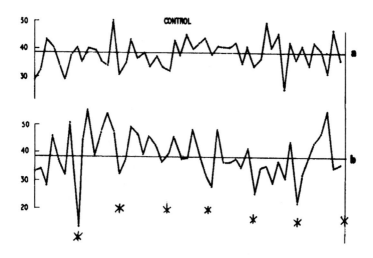

Figure 13

this? Even a perfunctory glance at the graph shows that there is a low reading at intervals of one-seventh all the way along the line. (Marked X—notice that 7 does not divide exactly into 51½, therefore there are two points in the graph where there is an interval of eight degrees.)

Further inspection reveals that the tops of these seven waves tend to have a cleft—this suggests that there are two beats—a 1/7 and a 1/14 combined in such a way that they agree on the down beat, to give the seven points marked, but that the tops to the 1/7 wave are cloven by the intermediate troughs of the 1/14 wave.

Further analysis reveals that the whole series is chiefly dominated by the fundamental 7th of the ecliptic (amplitude 10 percent) and by the 3rd (6 percent), 7th (10 percent) and 14th (10 percent) harmonics of that fundamental. That is to say there are four principal frequencies involved, the wavelengths being those which divide the ecliptic by 7, 21, 49 and 98 (=7X 14). Of the 180 possible harmonics only three in all—the 7th, 49th and 98th—reach an amplitude of 10 percent. (One ought to add, though it must surely be obvious, that there is absolutely no astronomical factor inherent in the Sun's motion which could account for this distribution—indeed no control is needed relatively speaking, for the Sun's mean distribution when treated in this way, is represented by a straight line.)

These findings, when seen with all their amazing implications open up a completely new vista into the science of astrology and reveal a viewpoint which is at once more scientific, more philosophical and far more beautiful—one which goes back to the very earliest and grandest concepts of the harmony of the spheres which inspired the great philosophers of antiquity.

We may briefly note now wherein Bradley erred in his approach. By starting with the generally accepted, but preconceived, idea that the only, or principal, division of the ecliptic was a twelve-fold one (or as we now see, the sixth harmonic of the ecliptic, six waves each with a positive and negative phase—it is this which composes the glyph of the sign Aquarius) and so adding up his totals in blocks of thirty degrees he thereby removed all trace of the smaller waves and left only those harmonics whose wavelengths were not obliterated by a thirty degree moving total, i.e., those of about $45°$ or more in length. The fact that these harmonics are substantially the same in Bradley's figures and those of the Association is revealed by the fact that the sum of these harmonics in both sets, as set out in the *Astrological Journal* for June 1960, show a very marked similarity. They are not identical however, nor are the short-frequency waves—this simply indicates that whilst American and British clergy have a great deal in common, they also have differences. That is what one would expect.

It was also assumed by Bradley and supported by the Association report that because the points of maximum divergence from the expected distribution verged towards the center of the sidereal signs that therefore the sidereal zodiac was upheld as against the tropical. But this is simply the "off-center peak" effect illustrated in figures 4 and 5, resulting from many waves being superimposed. In actuality, when each harmonic series is isolated, it is seen that the longer waves are evidently phased on the tropical zodiac (see, for example, figure 10) and that none is obviously phased on the sidereal, though at present it is too early to say how the high frequency waves are phased and the same is true of the unusual harmonics, e.g. the seventh.

However, one certainly cannot be dogmatic about this subject at this stage.

Before summing up there is one more thing which should be said. In this article I have tried to indicate that the significance both of aspects and position in the ecliptic is to be found in the consideration of these in terms of harmonic relationships. But I am quite certain that mundane positions (house positions as we should usually say) are similarly to be understood. I do not say this from inference alone—though I am sure that such an inference would be fully justified—but from the study of actual results known to me. This view is supported by the work of M. Gauquelin whose studies in the mundane positions of the planets consists entirely of revealing the long-wave harmonics of mundane planetary distributions (though it is not clear that he realizes this).

Thus the general theory affects every part of our science. Some of its principles may be indicated along the following lines.

1. Every point or factor in astrology (whether a heavenly body or a point in the mundane or ecliptic circles) *is ideally related to every other point by harmonic intervals, and the symbolic effects which flow from these harmonic relationships in human nativities may be measured in terms of the frequency (or length), amplitude and phasing of the waves associated with them in any class of horoscope.*

2. In this connection one may reasonably assume as a working hypothesis that the *frequency* of a series represents a quality or attribute, the *amplitude* equals the degree to which it is present, and the *phasing* represents its relationship to other factors.

3. It is important to understand that each harmonic series (e.g. the division of the ecliptic into 7 waves of 51½ degrees or the 120 waves of 3 degrees) is based upon the working of an ideal symbolic number which *immediately establishes every point in the series as of equal force and validity*, i.e., a wave does not appear in one place and die away in another—it is constant round the entire circle and only "disappears" in the sense that its effects may be counteracted at certain points by other series that are also in force.

When these principles and their corollaries are fully unfolded, it will be seen that they offer a means of explaining, correlating and harmonizing all the conflicting ideas and doctrines prevailing in the present chaotic state of our science.

They fully explain the perfect doctrine of aspects of which our present one is a mere shadow; they explain much of our confusion about house division and sign division; they offer an exact account of degree areas; antiscions, mid-points and a host of other phenomena. They point without any doubt to a reunion of Eastern and Western astrology and whilst showing that the former has kept alive important traditions which we have lost, they also show that in the East as in the West, they have lost the key to many of their traditions and understand them only in a partial manner.

They show that we are using only a small fraction (certainly less than 10 percent) of our potential and that the 90 percent we ignore constantly plays havoc with our judgments. They have a bearing on all the principal pieces of astrological research going forward in the world at present, such as those of M. Gauquelin, and Dr. Tomaschek on earthquakes. They reveal that the physicist with his waves and quanta, etc., is dealing with symbolic numbers just as much as the astrologer is and they even strike, I believe, into the heart of applied mathematics, into the mysterious region which the statisticians sometimes call, paradoxically, the laws of chance.

They take us into the light and beauty of a world of thought which Pythagoras and Plato would have recognized as their own and which must have many familiar landmarks to the modern scientist too.

Finally, by greatly multiplying the significant factors, by defining them much more precisely and by showing that the hitherto least recognized factors (the high frequency waves) are among the most important; *these discoveries make the scientific proof of astrology a very simple matter* and reveal what I have long believed, that the great (and terrible) problem which confronts us, is not the scientific proof of our science but the right integration of this incredibly potent branch of human knowledge into the social order. This is a problem indeed which calls for the greatest vision and faith.

Chapter 4

The Basis of Astrology, Part I

*Based on a Joint Lecture to the Astrological
Association with Peter C. Roberts*

After the last article there was rather a long pause before the attack was resumed. This is partly because I became president of the Astrological Association and then editor of the *Astrological Journal* in rather difficult circumstances, and this proved time consuming. It also was because astrologers generally proved very resistant to the ideas I was advocating and I felt some reticence about pressing the case.

However, in 1964, I gave a joint lecture with Peter Roberts to the Astrological Association and this joint lecture formed the basis of Part I. In Part II, I illustrate the approach more fully. The great difficulty was to get people to understand first the weaknesses of astrology as it stood, secondly the sort of improvements needed and thirdly, what the new viewpoint was and what it implied in terms of greater scientific cohesion for the science as a whole.

This involved a good deal of repetition of what had already been said while trying to make the underlying concepts clear. In some ways this article does not carry the issues much further, but in other ways it will be seen that the concepts involved were gradually settling down into a more unified picture.

J.M.A., 1976

We are all engaged upon the building of a science—a science which of course has a practical application as an art. But what are the "stones" with which this science is to be built? This is an important question, for before any science can be truly unfolded, so as to realize its full potentialities, *it must first be reduced to its fundamental concepts*, to the simple units of which it is really composed. This is absolutely vital; a man who tries to build up a science without first finding the real units with which it is to be built is like a man who must try to build a house out of the rubble from other buildings. Every time he picks up a brick he finds part of another brick sticking to it and probably part of the original brick missing, too. The pieces are the wrong shape and mixed up with other, non-essential, elements. They are not *flexible* enough; they help him but they hinder him at the same time.

One can find plenty of examples of this in the history of science. Until the true basis of a science is found nothing quite "fits" and each new discovery only raises fresh problems. Once it is found everything falls into place and each new discovery confirms what is already known.

* * * * *

Now let us consider some of our astrological building materials. First and foremost we have signs and houses, planets and aspects; these are supported by such things as rulerships, mid-points, degree areas, etc. and of course various sorts of directions and other predictive techniques.

I said "we have" these things—but have we? Before one can say that one "has" something one must be able to say what it is, describe it, define its limits and if it is made up of parts, say what the parts are.

What then of the *divisions of the ecliptic*—signs for example—are we happy about these? Do we know where we stand? Obviously not, for the tropical-sidereal controversy cuts deep; and if you feel no doubts on that score there are plenty of other problems. Our Indian friend's, for example (whose testimony we cannot ignore) have numerous other ecliptic divisions, such as Navamshas, lunar mansions and so on. If these are valid we are missing something.

Then *houses*; no need to labor the uncertainties here. There are plenty of problems about the quadrant systems; plenty, too, about equal houses. What for example is the true difference between equal houses from the Ascendant and from the Midheaven? And then why not equal houses from the prime vertical or the east-west meridian? All must have their symbolism.

But that is only a start. What about cusps as boundaries or centers of houses? And again, Mr. Fagan and others assure us that there are really eight and not twelve houses, and so on.

Aspects seem at first to be definite enough, but they are not really so. Even putting aside the important question of "minor" aspects, and glossing over the problem of "orbs" (for which we can do no better than propound quite arbitrary rules which seem "about right"), we are still left with the whole difficulty of *interpreting* aspects. Our rough and ready division into "good or bad" (or "hard or soft" or "harmonious or inharmonious") is really only serviceable for as long as one does not look too closely at it. In reality, just as each sign is not simply "good" or "bad" but embodies a definite *principle*, so too does each aspect embody a definite principle which can operate to our advantage (even the square) or disadvantage (even the trine). These principles are in need of clear delineation.

So one could go on. One could take each and every factor in use in present-day astrology and show it to be surrounded by a host of uncertainties.

Of course, those who practice astrology must make up their minds how they are going to deal with these uncertainties. They must, and do, adopt whatever plan of practical procedure seems best and most sensible to them and one admires them for this and is grateful that there are those who, despite the difficulties, manage to produce something really worthwhile and of value to their fellows out of this rather patchwork science.

Still, there is a time for taking stock of our deficiencies and for asking ourselves if there is to be found a means of *coordinating*, *simplifying* and *unifying* some of our present heterogeneous conceptions.

This is surely the great need of astrology today and there is reason to think that we are at last in sight of a solution.

Let us consider the results of a piece of research.

* * * * *

First some introductory remarks.

Most statistical investigations of astrology are concerned with periodicity—with regular repetition. If we decided to consider what astrological factors predispose to a long life, for example, we might examine charts of octogenarians to find a sign preference for each heavenly body. If, say, Sun in Leo appeared outstandingly prominent (figure 1) this would amount to evidence for a yearly rhythm. If Leo and Aquarius were prominent one would be dealing, in effect, with a six-monthly rhythm, and if four fixed signs (figure 2), then one would deduce a three-monthly rhythm.

But notice here that if the rhythm present in the data were a sevenfold one (i.e., recurring every 52 days) no examination of the sign totals would reveal it. To quote Claude Bernard: "What we think we know prevents us from learning."

In investigating the nativities of a large group of polio sufferers we considered all the rhythms which could possibly be shown in our data.

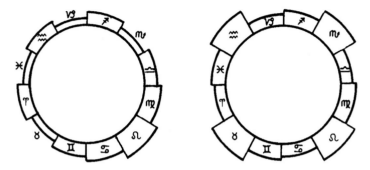

Figures 1 and 2

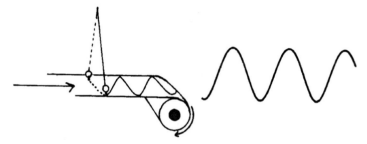

Figures 3 and 4

To follow our line of thought it is necessary to realize how different rhythms can be present simultaneously in such data. Consider some commonplace, everyday rhythms. A pendulum swinging to and fro would trace out a wavy line on a strip of paper drawn along underneath it (figure 3). Or a tuning fork, when vibrating, would trace just such a line with one of its tines. Similarly with tidal motion: if the level of the water at different times of day is measured and plotted against time, this same wavy line appears. *This wave is called a sine wave (figure 4) and the motions which execute sine waves are called "simple harmonic motions."*

Simple harmonic motion is characteristic of a great many entities. Radio waves, light waves and X-rays are all sine waves and electrons perform simple harmonic motion to produce them.

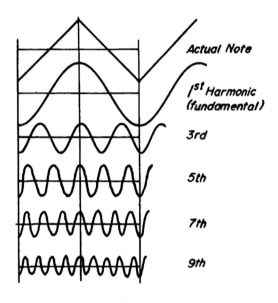

Figure 5

Sound waves are produced by the simple harmonic motions of the vibrating parts of, for example, musical instruments. But whereas a tuning fork produces a pure note, (a simple sine wave), other musical instruments produce more complex wave patterns—patterns which appear to be quite unlike sine waves but which are in fact just what would be obtained from adding a number of different sine waves together.

Some wave groupings give curious results; for example a violin gives a "spiky" effect somewhat like figure 5 and this is in fact a combination of waves whose frequencies are in the ratio 1:3:5:7 etc.—the odd numbers. In all phenomena of this kind the main note is called the fundamental and the additional notes are called harmonics. Thus if the fundamental is at the rate of 500 vibrations per second (a little below top C) then the second harmonic will be at the rate of 1,000 per second, the third harmonic at 1,500, the fourth at 2,000, and so on.

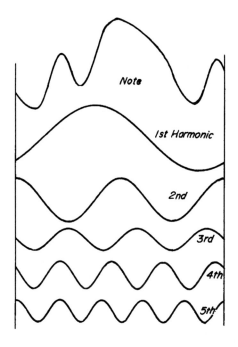

Figure 6

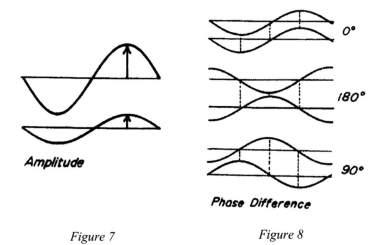

Amplitude

Phase Difference

Figure 7

Figure 8

55

Let us suppose that there is a musical instrument which produces the wave pattern at the top of figure 6. The note sounded by the instrument would produce that pattern over and over again. In order to find out what the component harmonics of this pattern are, we can subject the pattern to a process known as harmonic analysis and this will reveal to us the component harmonics (which have been drawn underneath).

This is usually done mathematically and the information obtained by harmonic analysis is the amplitude and phase of each harmonic present. Figure 7 shows clearly what is meant by amplitude; figure 8 illustrates phasing. If two waves have their crests occurring at the same point we say they are "in phase," if the crest of one coincides with the trough of the other, we say they are "out of phase." For other relative positions we speak of "phase difference" and measure this in degrees.

For example we could say of two waves which were exactly in phase that they had a phase difference of 0° and of two waves which were out of phase that their difference was 180°.

Obviously a random collection of waves would show all sorts of phase differences from 0° to 180° so that their *average phase difference would tend to be about 90°*.

Now the data we are going to examine consists of the Sun's position in the nativities of some 1,280 people who suffered from paralytic poliomyelitis. These 1,280 cases were drawn from three separate sources, 580 from Hospital A, 443 from Hospital B, and 257 from replies to a questionnaire sent to members of the Infantile Paralysis Fellowship. These three separate groups provided us with a means of examining our results for *consistency*, a most important consideration.

These solar positions are grouped according to the *degree of the zodiac* they occupied at the time each of these polio sufferers was born: so many cases between 29°30′ Pisces and 0°29′ Aries

56

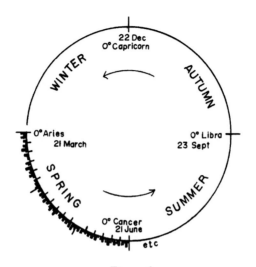

Figure 9
Degree by Degree Distribution

(these are classed as being at 0° Aries), so many between 0°30′ Aries and 1°29′ Aries (called 1° Aries) and so on all through the 360 degrees.

Consider these totals set round a circle representing the ecliptic (figure 9), the size of each blocked in degree showing the number of cases having the Sun in that degree. The outline of these blocks is a complex wave-form and can be resolved into separate harmonics. There are 180 harmonics required to completely describe the distribution.

We are concerned to find what rhythms appeared *strongly* and *consistently* in the data. All harmonics are present to some extent in any complex wave form; the really important or significant harmonics are indicated by *high amplitudes* together with consistency of phase from one set of data to another.

A full harmonic analysis was done by computer on the three sources of data separately, and the striking fact emerged that the harmonics which were multiples of twelve showed a higher amplitude and consistency of phase than any other series of harmonics. That is to say that the 12th harmonic (30° in length), the 24th (15° in length), the 36th (7½° in length), the 48th (3¾° in length) etc. were, taken together, of average amplitude larger than any other series—say the 9th series: 9th, 18th, 27th, 36th, etc. or, say the 13th series: 13th, 26th, 39th, etc. Furthermore the phase differences between individual harmonics in the "twelve" series were, when the three groups were compared, uniformly smaller than could be expected by chance.

The following table sums up the results. Remember that the number on the left includes, in each case, all the harmonics which are multiples of that number. Notice too that the mean difference of phase (right-hand column) tends towards 90° (which, as we said earlier, is the phase difference which would occur by chance), only the 12th sequence differing widely, with 69°.

One can see the point more clearly if one considers the harmonics up to say the 50th. Figure 10 shows *along the top row* the *amplitude* of each individual harmonic from the 1st to the 50th, and, along the bottom row the size of phase difference (the taller strokes indicating the smaller phase differences). It will be seen that the only three harmonics which have *both* a large amplitude and a small phase difference are the 24th, 36th and 48th (The 12th, interestingly, is not outstanding in itself).

There are a number of ways in which one could illustrate the striking consistency and strength of this 12th series of harmonics; the degree-by-degree pattern for a 15° or 30° run is very impressive but since we are limited for diagrams let us show the result of adding up the Sun positions (all 1,280) first for *all* the positive signs (Aries, Gemini, etc.) and second for all the negative signs (Taurus, Cancer, etc.) and giving the totals in 5-degree blocks. The result is shown in figure 11. There are six readings along each line, showing the number of Sun positions in the first five degrees, the second five degrees, and so on, for the positive signs (top line) and the negative signs (bottom line).

58

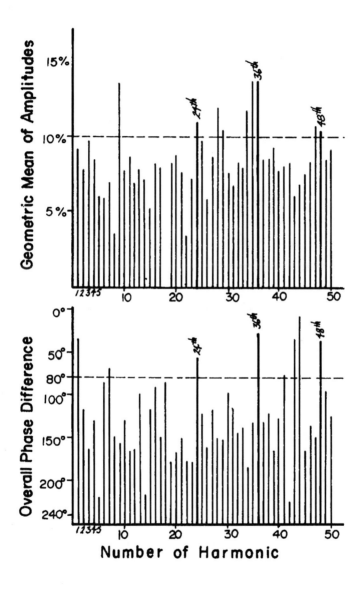

Figure 10

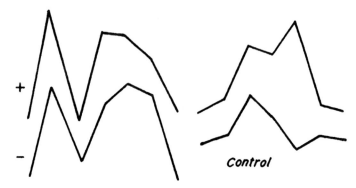

+

−

Control

Figures 11 and 12

| | Amplitude | | | Mean | Phase Diff. | | | Mean |
Seq.	I.P.F.	HospA	HospB	Ampl.	IPF/A	A/B	IPF/B	Diff.
5	11.4	7.6	10.4	9.8	70	103	99	91
6	12.8	7.0	9.5	9.8	91	94	68	84
7	10.5	8.1	8.9	8.8	83	104	71	86
8	12.2	8.3	9.6	10.0	66	79	79	75
9	10.5	6.7	9.3	8.8	70	109	113	97
10	13.3	7.3	9.6	10.1	72	113	97	94
11	9.6	9.4	9.5	9.5	74	111	85	90
(12)	13.4	7.6	11.7	(10.9)	67	82	59	(69)
13	11.4	7.7	10.8	10.0	115	85	119	106
14	8.6	8.4	9.5	8.8	60	89	86	78
15	11.3	8.3	9.9	9.8	62	126	101	96
16	11.8	9.7	7.6	9.7	62	92	78	78
17	12.9	7.8	6.1	8.9	76	98	87	87
18	12.1	6.4	9.4	9.3	92	73	85	83
19	12.5	7.8	6.7	9.0	81	131	65	92
20	14.3	8.1	9.6	10.7	81	128	87	99

The correlation co-efficient is 0.93; a likeness which would occur by chance only once in 100 times. Figure 12 shows the same

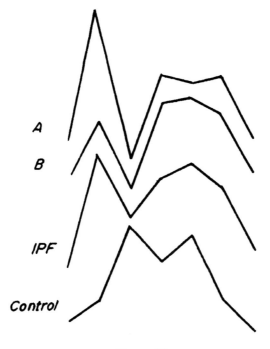

A

B

IPF

Control

Figure 13

comparison made on a control set of comparable (non-polio) birth dates. Here the correlation co-efficient of 0.04 is such as would occur by chance in about half of such pairs of lines.

For any statistically demonstrated feature to be valid, it is necessary to show that different sources of data show the same features independently. In figure 13 we have divided the data, not into positive and negative groups of signs, but into Hospital A, Hospital B, I.P.F. and Control.

Finally it is necessary to show that the departures from the mean value are greater than would be expected by chance. The individual degree totals for the 30° run (this contains all the 12th series of harmonics) depart from the mean to such an extent that this result could only be expected once in 1,000 times.

61

Where have these results taken us? Some of the results have no doubt been difficult to follow (and on this point it should be said that it is hoped to publish a more fully explanatory account of the work) but those who can envisage the implications of the results will see a new world of astrology opening up in front of them.

Chapter 5

The Basis of Astrology, Part II

The evidence which was gleaned from the analysis of the poliomyelitis nativities in Part One of this article now enables us to answer some of the questions which were posed at the outset.

To cut a long story short, it seems evident that all astrological symbolism (with the exception of the planets themselves) is, or should be, based upon the harmonics of symbolic circles of relationships. There are many such circles in astrology; there is the circle of the ecliptic around which the sun appears to travel and near to which the moon and planets circle their orbits. In the case of these bodies, they may be considered as having an ever-changing relationship to some fixed starting point on the circle. In the case of the signs of the zodiac we take the vernal equinox as the starting point, but there are other points which can be taken too. Each planet has a circle of relationships with every other planet, starting from the conjunction and moving round through all the aspects and returning to the conjunction.

Again, taking an analogy (though not a precise one) from the Sun's relationship to $0°$ Aries, we may suspect each planetary orbit of forming a significant symbolic circle of relationships with, say, its ascending node. And again the siderealists advocate a symbolic starting-point among the circle of constellations, and this may be, and probably is, true though the nature of this starting point is obscure. Then there are the diurnal circles of relationships—the cir-

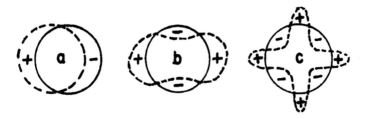

Figure 1

cles which each body describes in relation to the Ascendant, Midheaven or any other point which can be shown to have a real symbolic subsistence.

What is meant by the harmonics of such symbolic circles of relationship? It is quite simple.

If we take a point on a circle and say that this point has a symbolic value, that it is a symbolic center of activity or power—then we may consider the potential activity of that point in terms of numerical symbolism. If we consider it in terms of the number one then we are seeing it as the one and only positive point in the circle, and in this case the opposite point will stand in the relationship of a minus quantity. This gives rise to the first harmonic (figure 1a). If we consider our point in terms of the number two, in terms of all that is symbolized by duality, as subject and object and so on, then we have a second symbolic point, two positives with negative points in square to them. This gives rise to the second harmonic (figure 1b).

If we go on to, say, the number Four, then we have four points of similar nature, all positive, with negative points between them (figure 1c). One may, in fact, consider one's original point in terms of the symbolism of any number, and the effects which follow from the activity of that point in terms of that symbolic number will be seen as ebbing and flowing between the positive and negative phases round the whole circle of relationships.

64

"Stop, stop!" cries the reader, "This is too much!"

Fair enough; let us come down to earth. In a moment we will have some actual examples. What we are saying is that the nature and significance of astrological effects can best be described or considered in terms of number symbolism and once this fact is realized our whole language of symbolic divisions—signs, houses, aspects, symbolic measures, etc.—will suddenly come to life and be found to be capable of *far greater differentiation as to meaning*.

In order to make it clear what we are talking about, let us have some examples, beginning with the first harmonic. When collecting birth data of poliomyelitis, I was able to invite (through the pages of the *Infantile Paralysis Fellowship Bulletin*) such polio sufferers as knew their time of birth as well as date, to send me this data. In this way I obtained 256 such times of birth.

Thanks to the labors of some association members, the full schemes of these nativities were calculated and it is to the distribution of the Ascendants through the signs that I wish to draw attention. They were as follows:

♈	♉	♊	♋	♌	♍	♎	♏	♐	♑	♒	♓
4	9	15	21	34	29	40	35	31	18	15	4

It will be seen that we have a fine specimen here (figure 2) of the first harmonic—only four cases in Aries and four in Pisces, yet no less than 40 in Libra. Of course the Ascendant changes more quickly in the region of Aries and Pisces, and slowly at the opposite point, therefore we must have regard to the *expected frequency* with which each sign would occur as Ascendant. This is represented by the dotted line in figure 2. Even allowing for this effect, the first harmonic, with a trough approximately in Aries and a peak in the opposite sign, is clearly seen as the dominant influence—far more so than any particular sign.

It should be said that I believe this effect has nothing to do with poliomyelitis but reflects the way in which the data was ac-

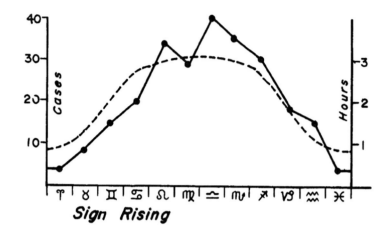

Figure 2

quired. Out of some thousands of people who might have read the article appealing for data, these were the few who were *sufficiently interested in what someone else was doing and sufficiently desirous of communicating themselves to that someone else,* to be prepared to get in touch. In other words they were a group of characteristically *altero-centric* people (the Libran side of the zodiac corresponding to the western or seventh-house side of the horoscope as opposed to the *ego-centric,* eastern or Aries side).

When we turn to the second harmonic there are numerous examples in the astrological field available to us. Professor Tomaschek has shown the tendency of Uranus to verge towards the upper or lower meridian at the time of earthquakes, i.e., to either of two points in the diurnal circle. (Though it should be said that the second harmonic alone will not of itself account for the observed closeness of Uranus to these points, other harmonics are evidently in force here.)

In America, Bradley, Woodbury and Brier, and in Australia, Adderley and Bowen have shown the importance of the second

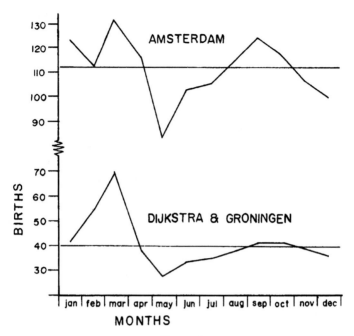

Figure 3
Dutch Lung Cancer Birth Dates

harmonic of the synodic lunar period in rainfall precipitation in their respective continents. (In England it is the first harmonic which has been found to be of significance in this respect—different countries, different astrological effects.)

In September 1963, B. K. S. Dijkstra, writing in the *Journal of the National Cancer Institute* (Vol. 31, No. 3) showed the abnormality of the distribution of birth dates of a group of Dutch lung-cancer sufferers. In the correspondence which followed the publication of Dijkstra's figures in *The Lancet* two more Dutch sources sent in similar data—(both claiming that they gave no support to Dijkstra's views!).

Yet if the three sets of lung-cancer birth dates: Dijkstra's, University College Hospital, Groningen and Cancer Registration

Center, Amsterdam, are taken, and the first two sets (totaling 480 cases in all) are compared with the third set (1,346 cases) we see that they precisely confirm one another and that the second harmonic of the solar cycle (but not the second only, since the first "wave" shows a higher peak than the second) plays a significant part in the distribution of the

Of course Dijkstra puts forward a theory based upon efficient causation (that of a Vitamin A deficiency in earliest infancy), but if the lung-cancer birth dates were to be treated in the same way as the polio birth dates examined in Part I of this article, would they not show shorter frequency harmonics which would dispose for ever of such theories?

(Again, English lung cancer birth dates also show the action of the second harmonic, without however the high peak of cases in March—different countries different astrological effects.)

To jump to the fourth harmonic we cannot do better than instance the splendid researches of M. Gauquelin, the French statistician (not astrologer) who has examined the distribution of planets *in their diurnal circles*. Figure 4 shows the distribution of Mars, Jupiter, Saturn and Moon in relation to the four angles of the horoscope in the nativities of two very large groups of famous men and women—French cases (11,000) on the top line, other countries (19,000) on the bottom. This diagram (taken from "Homme et les Astres") shows a coefficient of correlation in the order of 1: 100,000, and it is easy to see that the first and fourth harmonics of the diurnal circle determine the distribution (figure 5). (c.f. also, figures la and 1c).

What, now, can we say about the basis of astrology? Can we find some integral, unifying basis for all astrological symbolism? I think we can.

At present, when we consider the relationships of two planets to each other, we say they are in aspect when they reach any one of

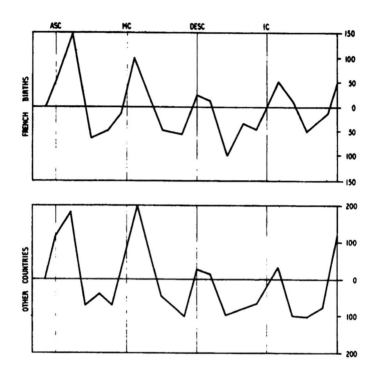

Figure 4

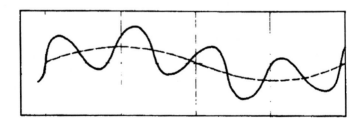

Figure 5

69

a dozen or so angular relationships, neatly spaced round the 360 degrees. But we should really get much more out of it if we could begin to think of them as always in some potentially significant relationship, a relationship which derives its significance from the number by which it was necessary to divide the circle in order to describe the relationship. The sesquiquadrate is three-eighths of the circle, the biquintile is two-fifths; they draw their meaning, basically, from the numbers 8 and 5. But why not an aspect of, say, ten forty-ninths?—an aspect which would derive its meaning, basically, from the number seven.

The point which we are gradually trying to establish is that it gives a false picture of what astrology is really about if we lay all the emphasis upon the number 12—12 signs, 12 houses etc. Every number has its part to play.

In discussing the famous *Birthdates of Clergymen* experiments which most of our readers will remember (2,492 American clergy examined by Bradley, and 1,972 English clergy examined by an Association Group under Brigadier Firebrace) I drew attention in the *Journal* to the outstanding importance of the 7th, 49th, and 98th harmonics of the solar distribution in the English clergy. At that time one had only a very incomplete picture of the whole harmonic scheme of this distribution but since then all this data (plus the control) has been subjected to harmonic analysis by computer and it was most striking to see that out of the long list of 180 harmonics of the English data, *three harmonies, and three only*, reached double figures in their amplitude—the 7th, 49th (7 X 7), and the 98th (7 X 7 X 2)! The significance of the number seven in relation to the priestly function is proverbial. (The American data, though it shows other significant similarities with the English data does not lay so great an emphasis on the seventh series—different countries, different astrological effects.)

One more example to show the high frequency harmonics. If we take the degree-by-degree distribution of the sun in the 360 degrees of the ecliptic in the polio genitures and cut it into 24 sectors

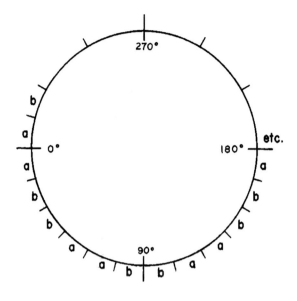

Figure 6

of 15° each, and if we make two groups of 12 X 15° sectors ("a" sectors and "b" sectors as shown in figure 6) and compare the Sun's degree-by-degree distribution in all the "a" sectors put together with its distribution in all the "b" sectors put together, then this is the result we get (figure 7).

I do not know what the co-efficient of correlation of these two distributions is but they are obviously telling the same story. This is like the "note" sounded by our musical instrument in figure 6 of Part I of the article. In the polio maps this "note" is "sounded" over and over again every 15° round the ecliptic. These two distribution patterns resemble one another because both are regulated by the 24th harmonic of the solar cycle and its sub-multiples, the 48th, 72nd, etc.

The 120th plays a particularly important part.

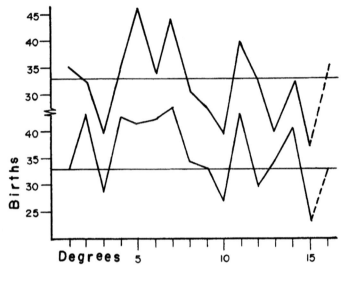

Figure 7

It must not be thought that this kind of thing applies to the solar distribution only; *every symbolic circle of relationships* in astrology can be treated in the same way.

Furthermore, by this method and by an understanding of the true symbolism of numbers, we should quickly arrive at a much deeper insight into the precise *meaning* of each aspect or aspect series.

Then consider the signs of the zodiac. These are especially related to the positive and negative phases of the sixth harmonic of the ecliptic (see figure 8), but we should do even better with our understanding of the ecliptic if we could remember, as our Eastern friends do, that there are many other divisions of the ecliptic, each drawing its significance from the symbolism of the number upon which it is based.

Note again, in this connection, that by looking at the divisions of the ecliptic in this way we shall arrive at a deeper insight into

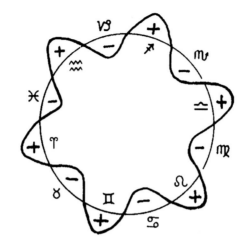

Figure 8

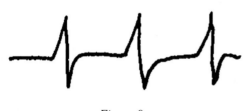

Figure 9

their meaning too. In the case of the sixth harmonic it is not just a case of six positive and six negative phases, all alike, but of a single six-fold or twelve-fold principle, *each step or phase of which has its own symbolism*; so that the first represents the impulse to life and the second the physical basis or means of life, the third the idea of relationship, and the fourth the expression of that idea in the family circle, the fifth the inner source of health and the sixth the health as expressed in the parts and so on. So with the divisions of the ecliptic by other numbers—say by 360—it is possible to relate each step in the series to an ideal symbolic interpretation, so that we know the meaning of the degrees of the zodiac, not in veiled symbols, but in their purity, as principles.

One more point; degree areas (as opposed to symbolic degree interpretations). Figure 9 shows an electrocardiograph; three heart beats in a given time. Each beat in this series can be viewed in the same way as our musical note sounded on a certain type of instrument—a combination of a number of harmonics, combined, in this case, to give one sudden leap, as it were, every so often. If then we regard figure 9 as the harmonics of the entire ecliptic then we have a set of harmonics which combine to throw up a highly significant degree area once every 120° degrees. Is not this the basis of our finding that the horoscope of say, actors, or sufferers from some complaint, show significant strength in certain degree areas—that their horoscopes are characterized by certain combinations of harmonics which render certain degree areas of outstanding importance?

A correspondent has written to complain, since the publication of Part I of this article, that I am trying to make astrology conform to the narrow concepts of materialistic science. It is true that the metaphysical world view of orthodox scientists is narrower than ours; it is true that they are gradually beginning to realize the connection between celestial phenomena and terrestrial events. But they are still at the most primitive stage of this realization. They still think that all they have to deal with is say, some crude effect in the earth's magnetic field at the new and full moon. But the picture is far too complex to permit of such simple, materialistic explanations. Only a symbolic mode of thought and language (through which phenomena can be related to noumena) will serve such a purpose. The scientists can never convert us to their world view which is totally inadequate to the situation—they can only adopt ours.

Chapter 6

Astrology and Genetics: Red Hair

Geneticists say that human characteristics are determined by the biological "genetic code." Astrologers say that the same characteristics are described by the "astrological code." It therefore follows that these two codes must correspond. This article is an attempt to begin the process of demonstrating that genetic types can be distinguished astrologically through the study of harmonics.

J.M.A., 1976

* * *

I always feel, upon acquiring a set of astrological data for statistical study, like the possessor of a treasure chest of which I still have to find the key. Being convinced of the intelligibility of our science I know that the data are capable of yielding up valuable information about astrological laws. The information is there, but may take some getting out. Fortunately a skeleton key now exists which can be adapted to all astrological locks.

In the course of many years of pursuing astrological research my experience has *always been the same in one respect*. I have invariably found that conventional astrological concepts and beliefs such as the signs (with their usually accepted meanings), the houses and the aspects, though they may be shown to have a basic validity, are *useless* for scientific purposes. Studies made in these terms produce results which may or may not confirm, in some degree, our traditional beliefs, but which, even when they do confirm them, can be rendered infinitely more convincingly and satisfactorily when the study is made in terms of the wider fundamentals of which our conventional signs, houses and aspects are simply particularized forms.

Some time ago I invited members to send accurate birth data of people with red hair. Recent years have seen outstanding developments in the field of genetics and I believe astrology is now in a position to link up with these developments and to distinguish clearly specific genetic traits in horoscopic terms. Red hair is an obvious genetic trait which is sufficiently common to make data relatively easy to obtain and sufficiently uncommon and definite to lend itself to study in these terms.

Ideally one needs several hundred cases but once one knows exactly what one is looking for a smaller number will suffice and the hundred cases of red hair which were sent will serve to demonstrate this. The key lies in the examination of astrological data in terms of the harmonics of cosmic circles.

What do I mean by cosmic circles? Every celestial body describes analogical circles. First, for example, we have the diurnal circle: the apparent circle which each body describes as the earth rotates and the body rises, culminates, sets and passes its nadir. This phenomenon is usually thought of in terms of *houses*. Second there is the circle which each body describes round the ecliptic, from 0 Aries (or some other point) back to the same point. This is usually thought of in terms of *zodiacal position*. Third there is the circle which one body describes in relation to another as it moves round from one conjunction to the next. This is usually thought of in terms of *aspects*. There are other circles but these will do to start with.

We shall return to this line of enquiry but first let us see what conventional lines of approach will tell us.

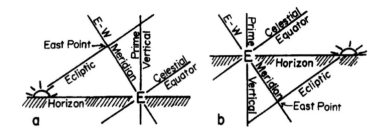

Figure 1

The 100 charts of redheads were very kindly made out on "3D" chart forms by Norman Blunsdon and I am greatly indebted to him for this. It enables us to examine what effect, if any, planetary positions have when they are near the prime vertical, the east-west meridian and the actual line of the horizon (as opposed to when they are longitudinally near the degree of the ecliptic on the horizon).

A diagram will illustrate what is involved. If we look east on a summer's morning at sunrise, the great circles, if we could see them, would be as shown in figure 1a. The celestial equator cuts the horizon due east. The sun rises to the north of east and the ecliptic is well above the horizon when it passes due east. The prime vertical rises due east and passes straight up over the head of the observer, i.e. through the zenith, cutting the ecliptic on the way. The east-west meridian rises due east and passes through the poles of the celestial equator, also cutting the ecliptic on the way at what is known as the east point. I have always thought it a pity that this was called the east point, for, as can be seen in the diagram the point on the ecliptic which lies due east is that cut by the prime vertical and not the one cut by the east-west meridian. (It may be of interest to mention that in about a quarter of our 100 cases these three points all fall in different signs of the zodiac.)

Figure 1b shows the positions at sunrise on a winter's morning.

Consider first, then, the signs of the zodiac on the four points: Ascendant, east point. (the point on the ecliptic cut by the east-west meridian), prime vertical and Midheaven. The following table gives the number of times each sign of the zodiac appeared on these points.

(It must be remembered that in these latitudes the signs from Cancer to Sagittarius *move slowly over the Ascendant and fast over the prime vertical* and that signs from Aquarius to Taurus *move fast over the Ascendant and slowly over the prime vertical*.)

	♈	♉	♊	♋	♌	♍	♎	♏	♐	♑	♒	♓
ASC	3	4	9	9	13	15	5	12	10	9	5	6
EP	6	9	9	12	6	12	3	6	11	4	11	11
PV	11	8	14	5	10	6	2	4	5	11	13	11
MC	10	6	13	3	6	11	6	10	11	7	10	7
	30	27	45	29	35	44	16	32	37	31	39	35

Not to beat about the bush, the only visibly significant feature of this table is that Libra is consistently low. This is in accord with tradition as far as it goes, for Libra would normally be considered one of the signs least prone to red hair.

Nor is there anything to be gained by switching to the sidereal zodiac. Any difference is marginal and both are equally disappointing (with the possible exception of tropical Libra). This does not surprise me. I have always found such exercises almost fruitless. One might speculate about these figures according to one's personal beliefs, but the figures contain little that is helpful.

Turning now to planets on angles the following table shows the number of times when planets were (a) within 2° and (b) within 5° of one of the angles, i.e., using that term to include the four points listed above and their opposites.

Eastern and western angles are listed separately, as are Midheaven and IC. Note that bodies within 2° of the points are *counted again* among those within 5°; the four cases of Venus within 2° of the Ascendant are the only ones within 5°. (The Ascendant on this occasion but not hereafter is the planet's own Ascendant point, i.e., its latitude is taken into consideration.)

		☉	☽	☿	♀	♂	♃	♄	♅	♆	♇	To-tal	Avg.
Asc.		-2° 0	3	0	4	3	4	2	1	1	4	22	17
		-5° 8	6	2	4	6	6	4	1	3	7	49	38
Desc.		-2° 2	0	0	3	3	4	2	4	1	1	20	17
		-5° 3	3	3	5	4	9	3	5	1	2	38	38
M.C.		-2° 1	1	2	0	2	2	1	4	3	1	17	12
		-5° 2	2	4	1	2	2	2	7	3	2	27	28
I.C.		-2° 0	2	1	2	3	0	1	3	2	0	14	12
		-5° 2	3	3	3	4	0	3	4	4	2	28	28
E-W Mer.	E	-2° 3	1	0	2	1	0	1	0	0	2	10	12
		-5° 5	1	4	4	3	2	2	0	1	3	23	28
E-W Mer.	W	-2° 1	1	0	0	0	1	0	1	0	0	4	12
		-5° 4	1	1	1	0	5	1	2	2	0	17	28
Pr. Vt.	E	-2° 1	3	4	1	2	3	1	3	0	1	19	17
		-5° 4	4	4	1	6	4	0	4	0	4	31	38
Pr. Vt.	W	-2° 1	1	1	1	2	3	0	2	0	1		12
		-5° 3	3	4	2	7	7	2	3	6	3	40	38
Totals		-2° 9	12	8	13	16	17	8	18	7	9	—	11.2
Totals		-5° 31	23	23	21	32	35	17	26	20	23	—	26.4

Here we have some interesting features and evidently some confirmation of tradition.

First the Ascendant emerges as the strongest point and, if we include its opposition—the Descendant—Jupiter, Mars, Pluto and Sun are all fairly strong here. Uranus also comes out strongly but it markedly favors the MC-IC axis.

Again, if we examine the totals at the foot of each column we see that Uranus, Jupiter and Mars are strongest within 2° of the angles and Jupiter, Mars and Sun within 5°. Pluto is not, over all, particularly strong.

Two other points of interest: Jupiter, on the basis of these figures is much stronger in the west than the east. This may or may not be significant. It is worth noting, too, that on the four occasions when Venus was conjunct the Ascendant it was a strongly fiery Venus, judged by conventional standards. Insofar as the hair may be taken to be involved with the personal beauty and especially in female genitures, this may lead us to look for a Venus involvement generally. (For example Mars was three times in Aries but 15 times in Libra!)

To sum up our findings on this topic we may conclude that:

1. We shall evidently be justified in paying special attention to Mars, Jupiter and Uranus as factors correlated with red hair. The Sun perhaps less so.

2. Mars and Jupiter appear to be strong in relation to the Ascendant-Descendent. Uranus in relation to MC-IC.

3. We shall be justified in giving special prominence to the Asc-Desc. The E-W meridian is definitely not implicated but there is good evidence that the, prime vertical is. The positions of Mars and Jupiter provide a good test. Mars and Jupiter near:

	observed frequency		expected frequency	
	-5°	-2°	-5°	-2°
Asc 12)	25	14	about 14 and 5½	
Desc 13)				
E-W Mer. (E) 5)	10	2	about 11 and 4½	
E-W Mer. (W) 5)				
P. Vert (E) 10)	24	10	about 14 and 5½	
P. Vert (W) 14)				

This strength of the prime vertical, (which almost matches that of the Ascendant) is especially significant when one remembers that the two are usually well separated from each other. They fall in different signs in 80 of the 100 cases.

So far these positions have only served as *pointers* to the factors to which we might attach importance. They are really of very little use in distinguishing the redheaded natus from any other. In singling out the cases where presumed significant planets are near to angles we are not only working on a very slender margin of significance but, what is much worse, we are constantly discarding the great majority of our redheads. *Much more comprehensive tactics are needed.*

Perhaps a word should be said about another conventional factor: degree influences. Maurice Wemyss (*Wheel of Life*, Vol. 1., p. 16-17) singles out 17° Taurus-Scorpio in relation to red hair. In these maps the area from 15° to 20° Taurus-Scorpio is not only not strong, it is below average in strength. Mr. Carter does not specifically mention red hair in his *Encyclopaedia of Psychological Astrology* and I would not like to try to judge exactly how significant, in this context, are the various degree areas he mentions in connection with hair generally. But their significance is not obviously outstanding.

But even if we were successfully to single out one or two degree areas the same thing would apply as to angles: the great majority of our redheads would constantly be left out in the cold. As I said, *one needs a more comprehensive yardstick.*

There are other features in these maps which one might discuss in convention terms—sign positions for example, but although one can find isolated items of interest they usually leave one substantially in the dark and are certainly no use as reliable tools for distinguishing between the redheaded natus and others.

Let us then see what can be done by examining these maps in a different way, and since we have just been considering degree influences, let us begin with zodiacal positions.

Let us leave aside the distribution of planets through the 12 signs, which are merely puzzling when baldly stated, and consider the distribution of the Sun, Moon and Venus within the signs. Here we give the number of times each of these bodies appeared in each 5° sector of all the signs put together.[7]

	0°-5°	5°-10°	10°-15°	15°-20°	20°-25°	25°-30°
Sun	13	13	22	26	10	17
Moon	19	13	23	18	12	15
Venus	24	10	16	17	16	18
Totals	56	36	61	61	38	50

These totals make a regular pattern: the two highest in the middle, then two low ones, the outside totals being higher but not as high as the central pair.

We can study this more closely if we list the number of times these bodies fell in *each degree* of the signs—how many times the Sun occupied the first degree of any sign, how many times in the second degree and so on up to the thirtieth degree, for all bodies.

	0	1	2	3	4	5	6	7	8	9	10	11	12	13	14
Sun	3	3	3	1	3	3	3	3	2	2	3	3	3	6	7
Moon	3	4	7	3	2	3	4	2	4	0	4	3	6	3	7
Venus	6	5	0	8	5	2	2	2	4	0	3	2	1	5	5
Totals 5° moving	12	12	10	12	10	8	9	7	10	2	10	8	10	14	19
Totals	57	60	56	52	49	46	44	36	38	37	40	44	61	62	65

	15	16	17	18	19	20	21	22	23	24	25	26	27	28	29
Sun	4	7	6	2	7	1	3	0	3	3	3	4	4	1	5
Moon	3	1	4	7	3	4	1	3	4	0	1	0	3	2	9
Venus	4	3	4	1	5	3	5	3	1	4	2	3	7	4	2
Totals 5° moving	11	11	14	10	15	8	9	6	8	7	6	7	14	7	16
Totals	69	63	59	56	54	46	46	38	36	34	42	41	50	55	61

[7] Mr. Blunsdon actually sent 101 maps but the time was not known in one case. Thus there are 101 cases except where angles and Moon are involved.

In order to see the general trend of this distribution pattern a 5° moving total is plotted in figure 2.

This distribution pattern (with a central peak somewhat higher than the outside one) is a common one. It simply shows the operation of the 12th and 24th harmonics of the ecliptic, waves of 30° and 15° respectively, both phased so that their highest points fall at 15° of the signs exactly.[8]

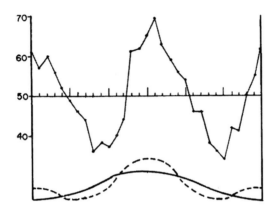

Figure 2

For comparison here (figure 3) is the graph, arrived at in exactly the same way, showing the distribution of the sun within the signs in the maps of 4,465 clergymen, British and American, from the *Astrological Journal*, Vol. Ill No. 2. It differs from the above in that the 30° wave is stronger and the 15° wave weaker. An exactly similar graph showing the same harmonics in terms of aspects (Mars-Mercury in 1.023 cases of poliomyelitis) can be seen in the same article.

---

[8] This graph and others like it is not conclusive proof of the validity of the tropical zodiac but the fact that waves are phased exactly on the tropical zodiac speaks for itself. Don Bradley's, conclusions in favor of the sidereal zodiac in his famous 'clergymen' experiment were based on an entirely false conception of the underlying factors at work.

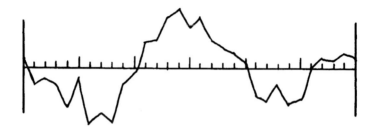

If the crude totals for the three planets are examined separately, shorter harmonics can be detected. The Moon, for example shows the common 3° wave (120th harmonic of the ecliptic) giving totals for every third degree of 30, 25 and 45. (A point of interest is that in a quarter of the cases Moon is within 2½° of 0° of the signs. A similar finding applies to the Ascendants of the charts.)

It will be seen that if the short harmonics, such as the 3° wave, are superimposed on the 12th and 24th harmonics, and those in turn upon the longer waves of the zodiacal circle, then certain areas will build up high peaks of significance. These are the basis of degree influences and could be demonstrated to exist in a particular class of map, from an examination of all the positions, even if one was unlucky enough to acquire a batch of data which did not, by chance, show a high total at those particular points.

The scientific basis of all zodiacal influences, including the astrological doctrine of signs and degree areas, is to be found in a study of the harmonics of the ecliptic circle.

The advantage of studying data in this way is that no case is discarded: every position contributes to the building up of the true picture of what is really happening. Furthermore, once the harmonic patterns relating to a particular class of map have been established, one is able to assess exactly any position in any map in relation to the matter under review in this case red hair.

There are of course other zodiacal harmonics in these maps which one might discuss but my object is simply to give examples of the principles involved.

Consider, now, what we usually call house or mundane position.

Many who read this will be familiar with the work of Michel Gauquelin as embodied in such books as *L'Influence des Astres* (1955). In these he analyses the mundane positions of the planetary bodies, that is their position in the diurnal circle, and in doing this he divides, as a rule, the diurnal circle into eighteen sectors—not 12 as with the traditional houses. By this means he is enabled to show the general outline of a planet's mundane distribution in a particular class of horoscope, the various professions and fields of human activity having formed his main study.

One common distribution pattern found by him shows a drop in the frequency of positions *before* the angles and high totals after the angles, i.e. in what we should call the cadent houses. Planets characteristic of the various professions are so often found distributed in this way that he has come to regard the cadent houses as "positive" and the cardinals as "negative."

I have never been exactly clear about the basis of Gauquelin's division of the mundane circle but the two pairs of angles evidently form the basis of his division. That is to say he starts with the four quadrants.

Let us now see how Uranus is distributed in the maps of our redheads on a similar basis.

Here I have made equal trisections of the four quadrants in each map and counted the number of times when Uranus falls in each. (My equal trisection is probably less satisfactory than Gauquelin's method but it is satisfactory for our purpose.) This graph (figure 4) shows the distribution of Uranus in these 12 sectors.

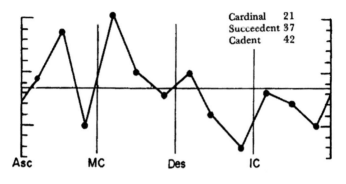

Figure 4

Even with such an extremely small total as 100 cases this shows a classic example of Gauquelin's "positive" mundane distribution described above. It is of course a combination of the first and fourth harmonics of the mundane circle.

This brings me to the first of two criticisms which I have always had of Gauquelin's methods.

Every harmonic series can be regarded as a *regular* series of waves and thus it must have *one point of reference* for its formation. This might be the Ascendant, or it might be the Midheaven, or there may be separate harmonic series based on each of them. But they cannot be based upon both at the same time because Ascendant and Midheaven are not a regular distance apart.

Let us look, then, at the Uranus distribution more closely. The following diagram (figure 5a) shows the distribution of Uranus in each 10° sector measured from the Ascendant.

(It will be noted that the points 90° away from the Ascendant are not now the Midheaven and IC for these seldom fall exactly 90° from the Ascendant.)

If we now take the distribution of Uranus in each 90° sector a remarkable correlation emerges. We here add together the two

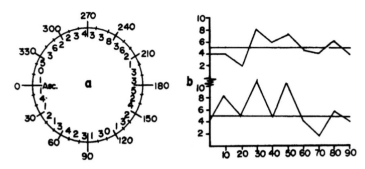

Figure 5

eastern series of decanates and compare them with the two western series added together.

E.	3	2	4	3	1	2	1	4	1
	1	0	5	3	6	2	2	3	4
	4	2	9	6	7	4	3	7	5
W.	3	3	8	3	6	2	1	3	3
	5	2	4	2	3	1	0	3	1
	8	5	12	5	9	3	1	6	4

These two distribution patterns are compared in figure 5b where their striking similarity is obvious.

This is a clear indication that there are harmonics based on the *Ascendant alone. But these have nothing to do with the Midheaven.* In 56 out of our 100 maps the Ascendant and Midheaven are either less than 70° or more than 110° apart. This difference is quite sufficient to put harmonics based on each angle separately out of phase with each other so that they could not possibly coincide or combine to produce high totals just after the angles. The only harmonic which can provide an exception, to some extent, is the 90° wave, the 4th harmonic of the circle, and the fact that this is the same (with a peak after the angle) for the 90° waves based on both the Ascendant and Midheaven separately, explains why the cadent

87

house do throw up high totals in figure 4. The successive 30° sectors taken in runs of three from the Ascendant give totals of 40, 34 and 26, and from the Midheaven 39, 36 and 25, peaks after the angle in both cases.

But because there are a hard core of cases where the angles are approximately 90° apart (so that these two waves coincide roughly to give peaks in the cadent houses) one should not on that account conclude that Ascendant and Midheaven are not separate and distinct factors, each with its own symbolism.

One can show this quite easily by examining the 30° wave which also appears in the relation of Uranus to Ascendant and Midheaven separately.

If we look at figure 5b one can see that the distribution of Uranus falls after the Ascendant and rises to a peak in the third decanate. In the case of Uranus' relationship to the Midheaven the reverse is the case. If we calculate the angular distance of Uranus to the M.C. in degrees and then plot the totals for all successive 30° runs put together we obtain the following distribution pattern (smoothed by a 5° moving total) in figure 6:

Again Uranus to the Ascendant shows a strong 5° wave, the totals for every fifth degree in this series giving totals of 28, 23, 23, 9 and 17.

This brings me to my second criticism of Gauquelin's methods, namely that by analyzing his figures in terms of 18 large sectors only, he can do little more than show the longest wave patterns—in fact the eighth harmonic (45°) is about the shortest that will show up clearly in his results.

It is no doubt good that, when the scientific world is so prejudiced against results of this sort, someone should take a sledge hammer and drive away with huge totals at one simple theme: the basic harmonics of planetary distributions in the mundane circle. But by ignoring the short harmonics of the mundane circle and ig-

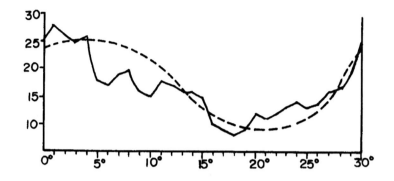

Figure 6
Distribution of Uranus in 30° Runs Starting
from the Midheaven (5° moving totals)

noring altogether the harmonics formed in the zodiacal circle and those formed in the aspect circles, he loses 95 percent of his potential material.

It is tempting to go on to show other planetary distributions in relation to angles—those of Mars for example form a distinct contrast to Uranus, but we cannot go into everything. To sum up:

The scientific explanation of the astrological doctrine of house and mundane positions generally is to be found in a study of the harmonics of planetary distributions in the diurnal circle.

Turning now to aspects between planets, exactly the same methods and principles can be applied.

A point of interest is that Mars, (in the Mars aspects I have examined) does not emerge as strongly as one would expect. Consider for example the aspects of Moon and Mars. One would expect to find something here, yet there are just slightly fewer conventional aspects than would be expected by chance and no obvious harmonics in the 30° series to be seen.

Such are the surprises one gets in testing theory against reality.

However, although there is no space to deal extensively with the aspect patterns in these maps there are plenty of features of interest.

One might use as illustration the aspects of Moon to Saturn and Jupiter, the two giants of our planetary family. The general distribution of Moon in relation to Saturn and Jupiter in these maps can be illustrated diagrammatically as in figures 7a and 7b.

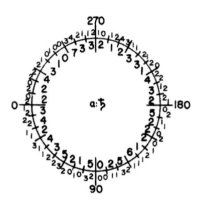

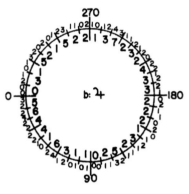

Figure 7

The small numbers show the numbers of times Moon falls in each 5° block measured round the ecliptic from Saturn and Jupiter, the larger numbers show the totals for each 10°.

The first thing to notice is a 45° wave, the 8th harmonic. Here one may give the totals for each 5° block recurring at 45° intervals, nine readings in each eighth part of the circle.

Saturn	9	12	10	8	15	12	16	8	10
Jupiter	7	7	9	12	16	14	14	10	10
	16	19	19	20	31	26	30	18	20

The distribution of Moon in relation to both planets shows a similar pattern and we are justified in putting them together to draw out the graph (figure 8).

But as well as a 45° wave there is also a 90° wave. Here we can count the 10° totals for Moon—nine readings in each 90° sector.

Saturn	8	12	18	11	8	13	10	6	13
Jupiter	10	13	18	9	10	14	13	9	4
	18	25	36	20	18	27	23	15	17

These may be plotted as in figure 9 which shows (1) Moon-Saturn, (2) Moon-Jupiter, (3) their combined distribution, and (4) the clear explanation of the distribution as the result of one 90° and two 45° waves.

It may be said and conceded that the present piece of research is open to the objection that no control group is used to show that these distribution patterns are not common to all human births. However, although it is almost certainly true that unrecognized

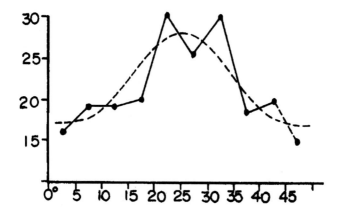

Figure 8

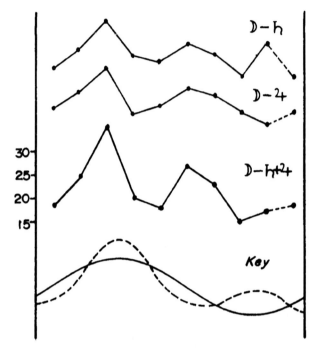

Figure 9

rhythms do exist in human births, one may take it that births generally do not show variations in relation to the aspects, of Moon to Jupiter and Saturn of the order indicated in figure 9. And the Moon of course has no tendency to form harmonic patterns of this sort in its angular relation to Jupiter and Saturn.

However, it is as well that we should consider the sort of significance to be attached to such results as we have obtained. It is highly unlikely that they relate to red hair as such. But red hair is a feature of certain racial types. One does not come across red-headed Negroes or Chinese. In a racially mixed society such as ours it is probable, or at least possible that long waves (the basic harmonic patterns) of the kind observed in this instance are characteristic of a racial group or some hereditary type of which red hair is an occasional, or regular, feature. (I have made some comments on this theme in the editorial of this issue.)

Carrying our study of Moon to Saturn and Jupiter a stage further, one may notice first that the Moon has a marked tendency to form other aspects to these two. Conventional aspects are well above average and these are partly the result of a strong 5° rhythm which gives the following series in all combined 5° runs measured from the exact aspect:

	0	1	2	3	4
Moon-Saturn	26	24	18	19	13
Moon-Jupiter	28	20	18	14	20
	54	44	36	33	33

Here we see what might be termed a 5° aspect, recurring every fifth degree round the entire ecliptic. A somewhat similar feature is present in the aspects of Venus-Mars, Venus-Jupiter and Moon-Venus:

Venus-Mars	26	11	17	23	23
Venus-Jupiter	26	8	18	19	30
Moon-Venus	31	16	21	16	16
	83	35	56	58	69

But to return to Moon-Saturn/Jupiter, it was whilst considering what sub-harmonics the 45° wave might break down into (the 5° wave is one) that I investigated the 9° wave (the 40th harmonic). Mars is generally associated with the number 9 and it occurred to me that the 9° wavelength might be significant in these maps.

Here is the result of Moon to Jupiter plus Moon to Saturn—40 X 9° runs round the aspect circle. (Both planets show a very closely similar pattern independently, as shown in figure 10):

One nine-degree wave with the third sub-harmonic (3°) superimposed. The Venus-Mars aspects show the same pattern.

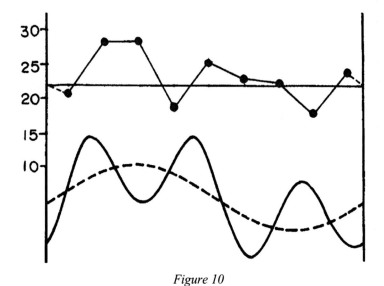

Figure 10

Enough.

The scientific basis of the astrological doctrine of aspects is to be found in a study of the harmonics of the aspect circle which each planet forms in relation to every other.

Summary

To sum up, there are a number of points which should be made.

First one should emphasize again that 100 cases is not many for building up the kind of picture we are trying to gain; one cannot rely on all the factors I have mentioned but enough are sufficiently well shown to merit confidence, having regard to previous studies made along the same lines.

Second, I have avoided technicalities and tried to explain in simple terms what is involved in this kind of study. It will be seen that what is really needed, if we had the resources which many sciences have at their disposal nowadays, is a large-scale study of the harmonic distribution patterns characteristic of the broad divisions of genetic types.

Failing this one might try to make a much more detailed study of the redheaded type comparing it with one or two other types genetically recognized as forming a clear contrast. In order to do this one would need a much larger number of cases.

If such a larger study could be made I believe it would not be too early to attempt the task of separating, from birth data alone, a group of redheads from a larger group with which their birth data had been mixed in a random way.

Such an operation would involve, of course, the use of computers at every stage. It would be quite impracticable on any other terms. It would be a very big undertaking but at least we have, I believe, the knowledge to do it, and the results might carry conviction in certain quarters hitherto unreceptive to astrological ideas.

Thirdly, nothing has been said in this article about the principles involved in the interpretation of astrological factors expressed in terms of harmonics. This is something which must wait for a future occasion and in any case one is rather at the speculative stage in this field, although certain tentative conclusions can be drawn.

Finally, it will be seen that the sort of approach to astrology indicated in the foregoing has the effect of unifying our concepts. The basic idea behind (1) houses, (2) signs and (3) aspects is treated in an integral manner and the scope of each is greatly enlarged and at the same time the three things are seen to be merely different aspects of one idea—angular relationships to (1) a point in the mundane circle (2) a point in the ecliptic circle (3) a planet.

When one carries out a piece of work such as the foregoing, there are usually a number of things which crop up which throw light on specific astrological topics not directly connected with the immediate object of the research. I should like to return briefly to some of these in future issues. The doctrine of orbs, for example, is one which merits attention.

References

The foregoing should be read in conjunction with two earlier articles by the same writer:

"The Search for the Scientific Starting Point" (*Astrology*, Vol. 32, No. 3, September 1958) and "The Discovery of the Scientific Starting Point" (*Astrological Journal*, Vol. 3, No. 2, March 1961).

The works of Michel Gauquelin provide abundant studies of the major harmonics of the mundane circle.

Chapter 7

Seven Thousand Doctors

In the *Astrological Journal* for Autumn 1969, Brig. R. C. Firebrace published a study of the birth data of 7,302 doctors of medicine and used these to justify what he believed to be the superior validity of the sidereal zodiac, following the methods of D. A. Bradley.

In the same issue I made use of the solar distribution of this large collection of nativities to demonstrate further the principle of harmonics and, incidentally, to point out that the conclusions he drew in relation to the sidereal zodiac were not warranted, for the reasons already explained in "The Discovery of the Scientific Starting Point" and illustrated particularly in figures 11 and 12 in that article.

At the end of this article I also gave some further thoughts on number symbolism in the context of harmonics.

J.M.A., 1976

* * *

In the past year Brigadier R. C. Firebrace has tabulated and analyzed the sun positions of 7,302 doctors of medicine extracted some years ago by Rupert Gleadow from the Medical Register of Great Britain (approximately 1850-1900).

The total number of doctors born with the Sun in each degree of the zodiac are a by-product of this huge labor and it seems desirable that these degree-by-degree totals should be given in the Journal as a future source of reference. They are set out below.

(Some errors which crept in when these totals were first given in *Spica* have been put right with the agreement of Brigadier Firebrace.)

In an article which we print in this issue, Brigadier Firebrace argues the case from these data in favor of the superior validity of the sidereal zodiac. In challenging his conclusion it may be as well to make it clear that I am not, in the ordinary sense, setting out to uphold the tropical zodiac. The tropical versus sidereal controversy is in my view something of a red herring, at any rate in its present form. There are more important things about the zodiac which must be understood and clarified before the tropical-sidereal problem can be dealt with.

My impression (supported now, after more than 12 years of study, by a great deal of evidence) is that our conception of the zodiac of the twelve signs is crude, almost to the point of being meaningless. The zodiac exists, but our understanding of it is inadequate. I have yet to see a single piece of statistical work (and there have been many now) dealing with the zodiacal problem which gives the slightest indication that the twelve signs, in either zodiac, are valid unities *in the sense that they are normally thought of.*

Figure 1, for example, shows a 5° moving total of the distribution of the Sun in the charts of 4,465 clergymen (Bradley plus Firebrace). The use of the 5° moving total is sufficient to show up local zodiacal influences. (I will explain the framed portions presently.)

Now it does not take a very exhaustive study to see that although there are areas of high and low frequency of Sun position, they have no visible connection with either zodiac.

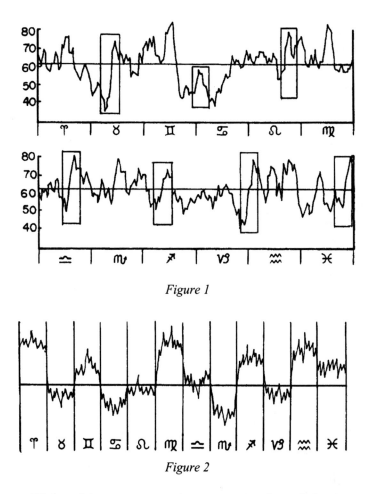

Figure 1

Figure 2

High and low sequences run across sign boundaries just as though they (the boundaries) were not there. This is indisputable.

If the signs of the zodiac were valid unities in this context then the changes from one level to another would coincide with the sign boundaries more or less, and once inside a sign it would not change greatly until it entered the next, somewhat as in figure 2. This (figure 2) is the usual conception today of the zodiac. It has been called a "box-type" zodiac: 12 boxes placed end-to-end.

But there is no evidence that this is what we are dealing with here. The really interesting changes occur, for the most part, away from the sign boundaries. Why, for example, does the moving total more than double between 9 and 14 Taurus (figure 1, frame 1).

This suggests that important influences in distinguishing "clergyman-ness" as indicated by the Sun position, are of a different extent, and possibly of a different character, to the 12 box-type signs.

The view which has been forced upon me by a long study of statistics of zodiacal positions, mundane positions, aspects and other astrological factors is that we are dealing, not with boxes, but with *waves*.

Furthermore, every piece of modern statistical work in astrology, including the work of Gauquelin, Bradley's meteorological studies, and others, confirms this fact, that it is waves—in fact harmonics of cosmic periods—that we are dealing with.

Let us look at an example.

In the case of the studies made of the birth dates of clergymen by Bradley and Firebrace, when Peter Roberts and I subjected these Sun positions to harmonic analysis (using a computer) one of the most outstanding harmonic series to emerge was the seventh harmonic and its sub-harmonics.

The seventh harmonic at work as a distribution pattern might be represented diagrammatically as in figure 3a or, when set out in a straight line, as in 3b; seven waves of 51°26′each.

But it was not only the seventh; in fact in the English clergy, produced by Brigadier Firebrace and his co-workers, the only three harmonics to reach an amplitude of 10 percent were the 7th, the 49th (7 X 7) and the 98th (7 X 7 X 2). Each of these is totally independent of the other two. The amplitude of a wave is the amount by which it rises and falls.

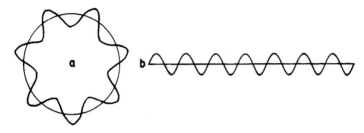

Figure 3

Now one of the features of the distribution pattern of the clergy (figure 1) is that every 51½ percent there is a sudden increase in total.

This arises because the 21st harmonic (the 3rd sub-harmonic of the 7th), is strong and phased alike in both the American clergy (Bradley) and the English clergy. And this 21st harmonic, together with the 14th and the 7th gives a "kick" to the totals every 51½ percent. These sudden rises, starting at about 10 Taurus, can be seen in the frames, drawn exactly 51°26′ apart, in figure 1. Of course they are mixed up with other harmonics and one (the second) is rather stunted.

The significance of the number seven in relation to religion and to sacred matters generally is well-known.

It is this fact of the coincidence of different harmonics in different classes of maps which is the basis and origin of degree area influences in astrology.

This is the first time in the known history of astrology that we have understood *how* degree influences arise.

(Incidentally, it may be worth mentioning that the most significant single harmonic in the combined American-English clergy is the 125th—a wave of only 2°53′ in length! If anything is significant in the clergy data, this is, strange as it may seem. We shall see the significance of this later.)

Let us now look at the Sun positions of the doctors. And here let me pay a further tribute to the industry of those who have given us this wonderful collection. A collection of a thousand examples of one class of map normally gives us a reliable basis for drawing general conclusions about that class. Seven thousand lifts the whole exercise on to an even higher level. We can see niceties here which would only be hinted at in a smaller collection.

It is difficult to know just where to start but since we are so fond of the signs of the zodiac we may as well start with the 12th harmonic, a wave of 30° in length which, as it happens, is one of the most significant waves in the collection.

We may conveniently see this by dividing the circle of the ecliptic into three parts of 120° each and giving one total for every five degrees of these three sectors taken together. In other words we are going to find the total number of cases between 0° and 4° 59′ of *Aries, Leo and Sagittarius*, and this will give us the first point on our graph (figure 4). The second point will be the total number of cases between 5°0′ and 9°59′ of *Aries, Leo and Sagittarius*. And so we shall continue until we reach the total for the last five degrees of Cancer, Scorpio and Pisces. Thus we obtain an overall picture of the Sun's distribution through the triplicities.

We do not have to strain ourselves to see the four waves of 30° each; they are perfectly clear and leave no room for argument. Whatever one may *like* to believe about astrology or the signs of the zodiac or the applicability of statistics to professions, the facts are there to see.

These are not really the signs of the zodiac; they are the 12th harmonic of the ecliptic; 12 waves of 30° each with a *peak and a trough* in each 30° sector.

If we divide the signs into two at 12° and 27° of the tropical signs (figure 4) the total number of cases between 27° and 12° is 3,478 and between 12° and 27° 3,824. This gives a difference of

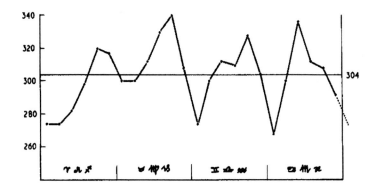

Figure 4

346 cases. The likelihood statistically of such a difference occurring by chance is in the order of *5,000 to 1 against*!

Siderealists who wish to give a restrained cheer that the peak of the wave occurs at about 0° of the sidereal signs may do so if they wish but the picture, as a whole, is still too complicated to permit conclusions of this kind.

The most outstanding result in the analysis by Brigadier Firebrace lies in the contrast between positive and negative signs in the sidereal zodiac. This of course is the 6th harmonic, a wave of 60° in length.

In order to have a good look at this we will divide the circle of the ecliptic into six sectors of 60° and give the total number of cases for the first degree, the second degree, the third degree etc. of all *six* sectors taken together. In other words our first reading is the total for the first degree of Aries, Gemini, Leo, etc., through the positive signs. The thirty-first reading will be the total for the first degree of the negative signs and so on.

This (figure 5a) gives us a picture of the distribution pattern (crude totals, no moving average) in a characteristic 60° run of the Sun's distribution.

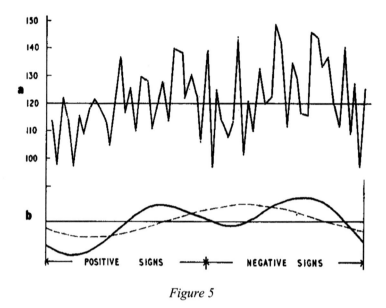

Figure 5

Again, there is no difficulty in seeing the 60° wave—the 6th harmonic—with a peak in the vicinity of 8° of the negative signs, a trough at about 8° of the positive signs and the nodes of the wave at about 23° of the signs. One can also see quite easily the 30° wave superimposed on the 60° wave, as shown in figure 5b.

If we divide the 60° wave into its positive and negative phases—adding the total cases between 23° positives and 23° negatives we have a total of 3,782, and for the negative half of the wave 3,520. This gives a difference of 262 and a statistical significance better than 1 in 300. This result is *entirely independent* of the 1:5,000 result for the 30° wave.

Siderealists may again claim that this wave, insofar as its nodes come near to 0° of the sidereal signs, is evidence in support of the sidereal zodiac. But the overall picture from these and other results does not permit of so easy a conclusion (quite apart from the fact that the picture of the zodiac, which emerges is totally different from either the conventional tropical or sidereal views).

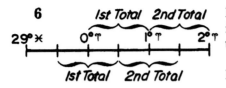

By adding this way the positive and negative halves of the wave are picked up.

But not by adding this way

Figure 6

If we look again at figure 5a we can see that there are very considerable oscillations and although these may seem to be mere chance they are in fact made up of other lesser harmonics, some of which reach very high statistical levels of significance.

As a remarkable example of this we may take the 2° wave—the 180th harmonic of the ecliptic.

Now this harmonic is the smallest we can find from totals given at one degree intervals round the ecliptic—and we can only find it if we are lucky and have, by chance, added up our cases so that we are more-or-less exactly picking up the positive and negative halves of the wave. In figure 6, if we add the total cases between 0°00′ Aries and 0°59′ Aries, and then between 1°0′ Aries and 1°59′ Aries we shall be exactly picking up the negative half of the wave in the first total and the positive half in the second total.

If, however, we have decided to add up our degree totals in such a way that our first total is centered on 0° (i.e., all cases between 29°31′ of Pisces and 0°30′ of Aries) then we shall be getting an equal score for both degrees because we shall have included half of the negative phase of the wave and half of the positive phase in each total.

As it happens Brigadier Firebrace picked the right point for his dividing line: *the tropical point 0° Aries!*

If we now look at the table of degree totals we find that the even numbered degrees are steadily in excess of the totals for the odd-numbered degrees.

Here is the amount by which even degrees outnumber odd degrees in each sign of the (tropical) zodiac:

♈	♉	♊	♋	♌	♍	♎	♏	♐	♑	♒	♓
0	+45	+26	+36	+24	+28	+20	+31	+5	+20	+1	+20

In every sign except Aries (where the totals are equal) even degrees outnumber odd degrees. The total difference is 256—again a level of significance better than 300:1 against chance.

This must be a powerful harmonic in these maps for it will be noticed that it shows up perfectly clearly despite the fact that our original data are given as noon positions for the day of birth.

We may now pause to notice that whereas, out of the 24 sign totals given by Brigadier Firebrace (12 tropical and 12 sidereal), only one reached a level of significance of 100:1 against, by treating our data in the above manner in the realization that all astrological effects are based on the harmonics of cosmic periods, we have already got three results at better than 300:1 against chance. And there are many other such results in these data.

It will be noticed that these high statistical levels of significance are obtained from these data despite the fact that the Sun's longitude, by itself, is only one factor in a hundred or more to which we give importance in the birth map. It takes no account of aspects, of other zodiacal positions, of mundane positions . . . And yet there are those who say that statistics are inapplicable to such data!

For generations astrologers have persisted, in accordance with a totally false conception of the nature of astrological effects, in adding up totals for signs of the zodiac, aspects within certain orbs, etc., *and in so doing have literally obliterated—one might say smothered at birth—all their high statistical levels of significance.*

There are countless revolutionary implications in this new discovery about the true nature of astrological effects, so many that we cannot possibly begin to discuss them here. It is not, in the writer's view, at all an exaggeration to say that they have within them the potentiality of increasing our understanding of astrology by *one-hundredfold*!

One particular implication must be mentioned. It is the revelation that we have become obsessed, to our great disadvantage, with the number twelve. Twelve signs, 12 main aspects, 12 houses and so on.

The fact is that although the number twelve does have a special importance because it is the lowest common multiple of 2, 3, 4 and 6, this does not justify the neglect of other numbers, all of which have their characteristic symbolic significance.

One more example will suffice to illustrate this.

In order to examine the 5th harmonic we set out our degree totals in five runs of 72 degree totals and by adding the total for each degree this will give us the characteristic distribution in a fifth part of the ecliptic circle (figure 7a). In order to see some of the significant features of this distribution pattern we next make a 5° moving total of the graph (figure 7b).

We can now see one feature with clarity: this is the 5th sub-harmonic of the series—five waves of 14°24' each. (We can also see the second sub-harmonic, two waves of 36°, but this is less pronounced.) This wave has an amplitude roughly in the same order as those we have looked at and which yielded very high statistical levels of significance. It is the 5th sub-harmonic of the 5th or the 25th harmonic of the ecliptic.

Turning up my *Encyclopaedia of Numbers* (A. E. Abbot) I find, under the number five, the following:

"Paracelsus affirmed that the perfect physician should master the knowledge of the five 'sects' of physicians for a complete understanding of the microcosmic man. He pointed to the significant

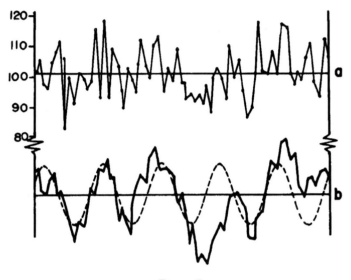

Figure 7

part played by the five in human illness, affirming that there are five types of illness, each divided into five further types.

"Doctors are becoming aware that the Five is also a critical number in the *development* of diseases, most diseases reaching a crisis on the fifth day, also during the fifth hour after midnight. In longer illnesses, the fifth week is critical."

From this it would seem that five and 25 have a special significance for physicians.

But we can go further than this. Five is (as the quotation mentions) the number of *microcosmic man*, and especially of man as the artist-soul at work in the cosmos. In this sense we may expect it to have a connection with all man's "arts" in the widest sense, and it is perhaps a number we may look for whenever we have a collection of birth dates of *men who follow the same art or profession.*

We must now be reminded that *the most outstanding single harmonic* in the maps of clergymen was, as mentioned earlier, the 125th—the 5th of the 5th of the 5th. Following are the positions of the Sun by degrees (Tropical):

	♈	♉	♊	♋	♌	♍	♎	♏	♐	♑	♒	♓
1	25	19	22	18	15	15	20	11	19	14	13	20
2	14	24	15	21	20	24	16	22	17	15	17	20
3	17	25	32	20	16	14	19	25	18	19	20	11
4	20	20	20	11	12	21	22	16	27	29	14	11
5	21	21	19	20	16	14	13	13	17	27	11	20
6	16	28	31	22	16	29	14	25	15	24	25	17
7	17	7	20	20	19	25	13	23	15	14	15	13
8	25	20	20	23	14	20	19	14	23	22	17	22
9	12	20	27	15	18	18	20	17	24	22	21	19
10	25	19	15	33	18	19	24	19	18	15	19	28
11	24	19	18	22	13	27	23	20	16	12	20	21
12	8	19	22	19	16	26	22	18	14	21	23	21
13	21	23	22	31	16	21	23	30	22	24	17	20
14	18	21	27	27	35	26	21	23	19	22	14	24
15	30	18	22	18	18	15	16	23	12	18	19	19
16	30	20	22	22	27	25	17	18	13	25	18	25
17	17	17	17	23	28	21	18	14	14	31	16	23
18	22	22	24	22	14	18	26	15	19	22	25	17
19	18	26	31	24	25	20	15	12	13	13	27	21
20	24	27	19	30	21	17	15	21	12	25	20	26
21	29	21	10	21	20	29	24	18	26	29	12	27
22	16	31	25	24	21	15	29	27	23	16	14	21
23	15	26	18	20	15	31	22	19	25	22	19	19
24	25	26	22	17	26	17	25	24	19	22	24	14
25	23	13	28	19	25	23	27	19	13	19	24	20
26	22	17	19	25	20	25	25	25	25	25	12	24
27	25	22	14	10	23	15	24	20	27	18	18	24
28	24	25	30	21	19	29	18	22	19	10	13	21
29	19	16	17	19	15	19	19	9	13	18	23	16
30	24	19	29	19	27	24	23	15	16	27	21	22
	626	631	660	636	588	642	612	577	553	620	551	606

Now in speaking of the numbers 5, 25 and 125 we say that the number is each time raised to a higher power: 5, 5², 5³. This is what happens, esoterically, when the action of a *number moves completely from one plane to another*.

Would it be true to say that the physician and the clergyman are both concerned with making man whole—but on different planes?

All the evidence is that the astrology we know and use today is in the nature of a vestigial memory of a much purer and more integral science which existed, perhaps, long ago.

The concepts we use: signs, houses, aspects, appear to be highly crude and formalized versions or remnants (adapted perhaps to simpler ages) of a far more subtle, flexible and penetrating scheme of ideas.

With the rediscovery of the true nature of astrological effects our study can enter into its heritage as a science.

Chapter 8

The Nature and Origin
of Degree Areas

The allocation of special meaning and significance to degrees of the zodiac (or to groups of degrees) has a long history. The subject has been variously treated according to the characteristic type of thought of particular periods of history.

In former times word-pictures were devised to catch, as it were, the symbolic content, on different levels, of a particular degree or degree area. In modern times men like Carter and Wemyss have made studies of different classes of map to see how far it was possible to deduce from them the strong degree-areas relevant to the feature in question—particular diseases, or professions, or skills and so on.

More recently Dennis Elwell using basically similar methods has brought keen psychological insight to bear in order to detect traits of character which cut right across all such boundaries and has done so with arresting results.

But in all these studies—at least those made in modern times—the precise basis of degree area influences was unknown. The problem of interpreting them was treated empirically: "we do not know *why* they have a certain meaning but at least we can find out *what* it is."

Today, following the discovery that all astrological effects can be related to the harmonics of cosmic periods, we are at last in a position to begin the task of interpreting degree area influences from the first principles of numerical symbolism with a full consciousness of the factors involved.

I say *to begin* the task, for at present the real problems are only just beginning to come into view—but that is the first step towards solving them.

In considering a problem most people like to have an actual example before them so that they can see the issues under discussion and an ideal illustration has recently been given us through the labours of Brigadier R. C. Firebrace on the dates of birth of 7,302 doctors of medicine. This large sample of a particular kind of map gives us an excellent example of degree area influences at work.

Figure 1 shows a 6° moving total[9] of the distribution of the Sun in the nativities of 7,302 doctors. (The 6° moving total is chosen to smooth the line a little and in particular to cut out several short waves, including the 2° wave, which between them cause considerable local oscillation.)

We can see in this distribution pattern that there are peak areas for the Sun's place in the ecliptic, as well as areas where it is less likely to appear, in the nativities of doctors of medicine—at least in those doctors born in the latter half of the nineteenth century and trained in the traditions of the schools of orthodox medicine in the United Kingdom.

In order to find out how the pattern changes with the passage of time one should examine a further sample from the 20th century; to find but how the pattern differs from that found among medical practitioners in other countries or other medical traditions

---

[9] A moving total looks the same as a moving average. To convert to a moving average, divide the numbers down the left-hand side by 6.

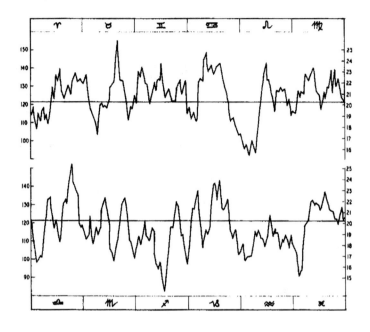

Figure 1

one would need samples of their nativities. They will change, they will differ, if only slightly, because events and conditions in time and space are always in a state of flux. But by studying such changes and differences *one may be able to arrive at the principles underlying those changes and differences*.

If we look at the distribution pattern in the graph we can see certain features straight away, some of which give the lie to, and others which uphold, present astrological beliefs.

1. The effect of the Sun's passage through the conventional signs of the zodiac (whether tropical or sidereal) is not obvious and the peaks and troughs in our graph seem to take no notice of the sign boundaries. As a matter of fact there are features which recur every 30° or 60° as we shall show, but they have to be sorted out

and they are by no means the only significant features. Nor do they conform to the current conception of the nature of the zodiacal signs.

2. The conventional notion that degree area influences are of great power and throw up huge totals of planetary positions in certain classes of map is false. The very highest peak in this graph is not six times the average for that degree, nor yet double the average, nor is it 50 percent above average; it is less than one-third above average.

When Brigadier Firebrace began the task of counting the totals for each degree of the zodiac in these maps he says he provisionally fixed on something like 80 cases for certain degrees as what he looked to find in confirmation (or otherwise) of the theory of degree area influences. This, or something higher, is the sort of figure which most students would have looked for in this case.

Yet the highest single total for any degree was 35!

This is an example of how present-day astrology exaggerates certain ancient truths of which it has retained some memory, in compensation for the fact that it has completely lost many others.

What distinguishes one type of map from another is a *large number of small differences*, not a few big ones. (It is this fact which has made the statistical demonstration of astrological truths such a hard nut to crack.)

3. We can say in general terms that for every degree area which specifically promotes a certain attribute, skill, quality and so on, there is another degree-area which specifically *militates against it*.

These negative degree areas, as we may call them, have not been studied to any great extent. Yet they are just as significant as the positive degree areas. We are now in a position to begin locating and interpreting them.

4. In general terms degree area influences are regarded as tending to recur at certain intervals round the ecliptic. Often opposition points are said to have a similar significance (we shall deal with those shortly), but sometimes they recur at other intervals, such as 120°: Carter gives 5° of the fire signs as having a connection with hair, for example. Similarly, every 60°, he gives 22° of the negative signs as connected with medical ability.

We are now in a position to see how this comes about and the particular instance last given provides us with an opportunity to examine the thing closely at first hand. Clearly, a factor which comes at 22° of the negative signs must be due to effects which recur every 60°. We can therefore take all six of the 60° runs, each comprising one positive and one negative sign and *put them all together* into one typical 60° distribution pattern.

We do this by adding the total number of cases in the first degree of the positives (this gives us the first point on our graph) then in the second degree, the third and so on. Our thirty-first reading will be the total number of cases in the first degree of the negative signs and our sixtieth and last reading will be the last degree of the negatives. Figure 2a shows the actual distribution pattern in this typical 60° series. (We are now dealing with crude totals for each degree and not a moving total as in figure 1.)

Now it will be seen that the highest total for any four consecutive degrees in the whole series comes between 19°0′ and 23°0′ of the negatives and the highest total for any three consecutive degrees comes between 19°0′ and 22°0′ of the negatives.

This is pretty good confirmation of the degree area empirically discovered by Carter. (The highest degree peak on our graph actually comes at 22° Taurus, although the crude degree totals do not show this degree to be the highest degree, its strength lies in the run of high scores between 19° and 24° Taurus—see *The Astrological Journal*, Autumn 1969, p. 21.)

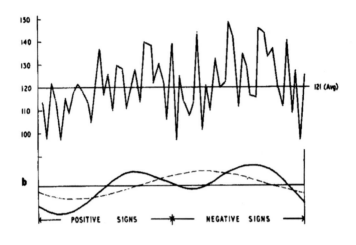

Figure 2

We may now ask ourselves why 22° negatives is so high.

Without at present going into the deeper reasons (which are admittedly the most important) we may say that it is because this is the point in the series where many of the sub-harmonics of this, the sixth harmonic of the ecliptic, coincide in their positive phase (the rising half of the wave) to *build up* a high peak.

To begin with, the first or fundamental harmonic (the wave of 60°), which appears to peak at about 8° negatives, is still just in its positive phase (the descending node being at about 23° negatives). The second sub-harmonic (30°) peaks at about 20° of each sign. The combination of these two gives us our basis (figure 2b).

On this basis other sub-harmonics build up at about 20°-21° of the negatives to give us our high-scoring degree area.

In order to find out what the *possible* harmonics of a particular sector of the ecliptic are one must, of course, divide that sector by whole numbers. The 2nd harmonic of our 60° sector is 30° in length, the 3rd will be 20°, the 4th 15°, the 5th 12°, the 6th 10° and

116

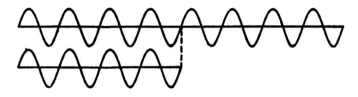

Figure 3

so on down to the 30th, which will be 2°. But of course only a few of these will play a significant part in the Sun position of doctors; to find out *which* is the purpose of our harmonic analysis.

5. One of the common beliefs about degree area influences is that they tend to form polarities, i.e. that opposite degrees of the zodiac are of like meaning.

Now when we say that opposite degrees of the zodiac are of like meaning we are, in effect, saying that there is a pattern which repeats every 180°—just in the way that the pattern we have been examining repeats every 60°.

We are therefore cutting the complete circle in half (in this case it is the circle of the ecliptic, but exactly the same principle applies to other circles: the mundane circle, the aspect circle) and observing a duplication of distribution pattern in each half.

But if we cut any complete harmonic series in half and compare the two halves, *one of two things must always happen*: If the harmonic series is *even-numbered* the pattern in the two halves will exactly *agree*, as in figure 3 where the *eight* original waves are cut in half and the second half compared, underneath, with the first half. We can see that the peaks and troughs *coincide*. (This will apply to any *combination* of even-numbered harmonics as well as to a single even-numbered harmonic.)

If however the harmonic is an *odd-numbered* harmonic and the series is cut in half, the two halves will be a *mirror-image* of

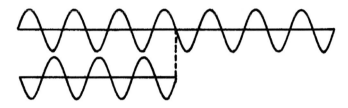

Figure 4

each other, as in figure 4, where the *seven* original waves are cut in half and the second half compared with the first half. The peaks reach up from the bottom line to meet the troughs coming down from the top line.

This will hold true at whatever points the circle is cut in half. It will also hold true for *all* odd-numbered harmonics—the first, the 5th, the 105th, the 1,005th—or any *combination* of odd-numbered harmonics.

Now every number is either odd or even and whenever we cut a circle of harmonics in half we shall always find that (1) in so far as the distribution pattern is dominated by even-numbered harmonics then opposite points will be of *like* nature; (2) in so far as it is dominated by odd-numbered harmonics opposite points will be of *opposite* nature; and (3) in so far as it is a mixture of odd and even they will be partly alike, partly opposite.

But there are the same number of odd and even numbers and the two classes of harmonics will presumably occur with equal frequency in the whole scheme of things—although in one particular type of map one class of harmonics may predominate.

In the case of doctors, for example, even-numbered harmonics might be found to predominate, for doctors are much concerned with the *body*, and even numbers certainly represent body, or the vehicle of manifestation (on whatever level), just as odd numbers represent that which manifests through body (on whatever level).

But when we study such a thing as medical ability (or at any rate the tendency to become a doctor) we shall generally find that we are dealing with a complex of different factors, just as one would expect, represented by the different harmonics. (If this were not so then there could be no degree areas for medical ability, for degree areas are produced by the coincidence of a number of different harmonic frequencies.) Among these we shall certainly find both odd and even numbered harmonics mixed together.

In the case of doctors, for example, we know that the sixth harmonic and its sub-harmonics are strong and these must all be even-numbered harmonics of the ecliptic circle because all the sub-harmonics of the sixth must be multiplied by six to give their number as harmonics of the complete circle.

Thus we can actually see, if we look at figure 1, that the line of the graph is *always* higher at about 20° of the negative signs than it is at about 7° of the positive signs. And this applies to the last six signs as well as to the first six, *because even harmonics give the same pattern in both halves of a circle*.

But we know that there are strong odd-numbered harmonics present in this distribution pattern too. We have referred elsewhere, for example, to the *25th harmonic* in these Sun positions of doctors.

Now an odd-numbered harmonic will always produce a mirror image in opposite halves of the circle. In figure 1, therefore, I have drawn in vertical bars wherever this mirror image is to be seen chiefly as a result of the operation of the 25th harmonic. These vertical lines are drawn at intervals of 14°24′—the wave length of the 25th harmonic. Time and again we can see the peaks reaching up from the bottom half to meet the troughs coming down from the top half.

We can safely say that in at least nine out of ten of all degree area influences wherever opposite degrees are said to be of broadly

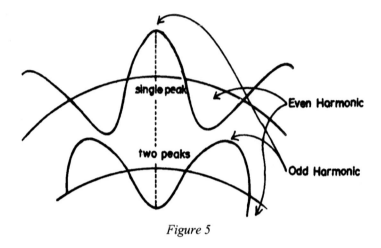

Figure 5

similar meaning, *one end of the polarity will always be stronger than the other*.

We can go further than this. Whenever even-numbered harmonics (such as the 30° and 60° waves) are at work producing important areas of similar meaning on opposite sides of the zodiac, if there are also significant odd-numbered harmonics present (as will usually be the case) one side of the zodiac will give a. single important area whilst the opposite pole will show two important areas, one on each side of the point opposite the original degree area (see figure 5).

One can see this happening again and again in our graph (figure 1). For example the three highest peaks, at 22° Taurus, 12° Cancer and 23° Libra are *all reflected at the opposite point in the zodiac by a trough, with peaks on either side of the central opposition point.*

All the foregoing items considerably extend our knowledge and understanding of the whole subject of degree area influences.

There are other things we can now tell about degree areas which we could not tell before:

6. How wide an area of the ecliptic does a degree area cover?

Because degree areas are a building up of harmonics at certain points, shorter waves being carried on the backs of longer ones, we can say in general that the higher the peak goes then the smaller its point will be (see the peak at 22° Taurus). Nevertheless we can see, in figure 1, some pretty solid highs as in the middle decanate of Cancer, and we shall be able to judge of the width of this (or any) area from a knowledge of the harmonics involved.

7. How quickly, and by how much, does the characteristic influence of a degree area fall off when one moves away from the area?

This again we shall now know how to judge. Sometimes (as between 11° and 17° Leo) the rise is rapid and large; at other times it is small and gradual. There is no one answer.

8. How much strength and importance should we attach to a degree area?

We have already mentioned this. The short answer is less than we thought. If we are looking for medical ability, for example, and find a planet in a medical degree we would, formerly, have been inclined to give it 10 points, metaphorically at least; in fact we should score it perhaps a half point.

But all this fades into insignificance beside the fact that we now know how to take any point on the ecliptic and give it a score, plus or minus, for medical ability (in relation, of course, to a particular planet).

9. It should be mentioned here that the idea of degree area influences, as usually applied to areas of the *ecliptic* is most certainly valid for, and should be applied to, *aspect* degree area influences and degree area influences in the mundane circle (the houses). Exactly the same principles apply to all three factors.

The harmonic patterns formed by the response of one planet to another in the aspect circle, or of a planet to, say, the Ascendent in the mundane circle, have the same tendency to form peaks and troughs in certain parts of the circle of aspects and houses as happens with certain degree areas in the ecliptic.

These peaks and troughs will no more tend to coincide with the exact (conventional) aspect points or with the house cusps than the peaks of degree-area influences tend to fall, say, in the exact centre of the signs. (In short our conception of astrological aspects and houses is every bit as crude as is our conception of the signs of the zodiac. The same, I believe, applies to progressed aspects; however we will draw a veil over this particular nightmare for the time being.)

We ought now to come to the deeper issues of how these harmonics arise and of how they are to be interpreted.

When I first sat down to write this article, the heading I wrote at the top was "The nature, origin and significance of degree influences." However, it seems presumptuous to include a reference to the significance when we are only just beginning to feel our way in the subject.

Nevertheless there are certain things which can be said, at any rate tentatively, although it seems wisest at this stage to confine oneself to very general statements.

In the first place, there must always be an active agent or, more properly, two—from the interaction which the effects, represented by the harmonics, originate.

In the case of the *circle of aspects* through which one planet passes on its journey from one conjuction with another planet to its next conjunction therewith, it is easy to see what the two factors involved are; obviously they are the two planets concerned; we know where we stand.

In the case of harmonics which relate to a planet's position in the ecliptic we do not know where we stand so far as interpretation is concerned, and shall not know until much more evidence is collected and imaginatively examined. The reason is that we can recognise only one of the two factors involved.

In figure 1 we are dealing with the relationship of the Sun to another unknown point or points. *What is that second point?*

There is a chance (an outside chance, perhaps, but still a chance) that the second point is a fixed star or other source of cosmic energy such as the galactic centre. Or it may be the so-called solar apex, the point in space toward which our solar system is moving. In all these cases our second point will show *precession* and by examining two sets of data of the same thing (doctors for example) from periods of 50 years or so apart, we shall be able to ascertain if the phase-angle of our harmonics is shifting by the rate at which precession takes place. This at least will tell us whether or not our second point belongs to this class of phenomena.

However, it may be—and this must still be the most likely possibility—that our second point is represented by the axis 0 Aries-Libra.

This possibility focuses our attention on those points in astrology (of which there are a good many) which are not marked by the presence of a particular heavenly body but nevertheless represent some point of astrological potency. Such points will always be the focus of some primary attribute, motion or relationship of a cosmic reality.

For just as each man is a unity and acts, first and foremost as a unity, yet each of his faculties has its own relative unity which is a source of activity, so each heavenly body has both a single unity and also a number of primary attributes or motions each of which represent stable modes of activity; and these, in the physical world, will have various energy fields related to them.

In this sense, for example, the line where two planes of activity intersect will give points *at which the significance of one plane can act into and upon another*.

If we picture two circles intersecting along a line AB, then A and B become significant points in both circles. (Although this seems so obvious one notices that it is a fact which is sometimes lost sight of in astrology.) This principle gives us all such points as the Ascendant, Midheaven, 0° Aries and many others.

It is this sort of point which may give us our second factor, the reaction of the Sun which produces the harmonics to be seen in figure 1. But there may be more than one factor at work. In fact we can say with certainty that there will be more than one. The other factors I have mentioned (such as fixed stars), simply because they are cosmic realities with their own activity must also be potential stimuli of harmonic effects, *though whether they can be of significant strength in the individual natus is another matter*.

All in all we may have a lot of trouble sorting out these forces. We are not likely to make much progress until we have a clearer grasp of cosmic symbolism, on different levels and until we have also mastered the basic symbolism of number.

This brings us to the final point.

It would seem to be obvious that the harmonics of the various circles of relationship in astrology represent symbolically the activity of the related factors according to the significance of the number upon which each harmonic is based.

Anyone brought up in the present-day climate of astrological thought might be forgiven for thinking the symbolism of number a pretty vague affair. It is not. The distinction between one number and another is ideally absolute and precise.

We are of course dealing with *ideal* numbers and not with the numbers of common arithmetic. The distinction of course is that in common arithmetic the number 8, for example, consists of eight units whereas the number 8, ideally represents a single eightfold principle, just in the way that the zodiac is a single twelvefold principle from which no part (strictly speaking it has no parts) can be taken away without destroying the significance of the whole.

It is upon a deeper understanding of the symbolism of these ideal numbers, in relation to the world order, macrocosmic and microcosmic, that the development of this new vision of astrological truth depends.

Chapter 9

Harmonics and Hindu Astrology, Part I

A year ago, while discussing the problem of the practical applications of harmonic analysis John Addey happened to mention to me that the principle of harmonics was evidently discernible in the Hindu astrological tradition. A cursory study of Hindu astrological manuals quickly revealed that Mr. Addey's hunch was not only correct but that this aspect of Hindu astrology, the Shodasavargas or 16 divisions, was already fairly widely known in the west in certain of its forms.

Anyone who has looked at any Hindu astrological literature will have noticed that charts are usually presented in two forms side by side: the radical, Rasi or sign chart, and the *Navamsa* or ninth division, chart. The excellent *Astrological Magazine* (1) always abounds in such charts. This second, Navamsa, chart, derived from the first, is considered very important and most predictions are based on a thorough scrutiny of the positions of the planets in the Navamsa and almost all books on predictive astrology make constant reference to this important system (2,9). A study of this second chart complete with the necessary conversion tables appeared in the first volume of the *Journal* (3).

These 16 forms of division, the Shodasavargas, of which the Navamsa is one, are used for:

(a) finding the positional strength of a planet.

(b) making predictions.

Which divisions are used for which is a matter of choice often depending upon the prevailing custom (4).

The divisions are commonly considered divisions of the *signs* by various numbers. These numbers are 2, 3 (the familiar decanate division), 4, 5, 6, 7, 8, 9—the Navamsa, 10, 11, 12, 16, 30, 60 and 150. The sign itself is considered the first of the Shodasavargas.

In the Navamsa system all the signs are each divided into nine segments of 3°20′ length. Starting with 0 Aries the first 3°20′ is said to be ruled by Aries, the second 3°20′ by Taurus, the third by Gemini, and so on, following the order of the signs through until at 10 Taurus one begins with Aries again. Continuing in this *way the full cycle of the 12 zodiacal rulerships are repeated nine times in the full circle.*

To convert the radical chart into the Navamsa form all that we need to do is to discover which divisions the radical positions are in and translate their positions accordingly. Full tables are issued with this number of the *Journal* but for those not familiar with this idea an example will suffice to show the method of calculation involved.

In the radical chart the Sun is at 6°50′ Aries and the Moon at 16°42′ Taurus. What are these bodies positions in the Navamsa chart? The first 3°20′ of Aries is ruled by Aries, the next by Taurus, and the next, beginning at 6°40′, in which the Sun is placed, is ruled by Gemini. The Sun is 10′ into this section. Since the Navamsa is one-ninth of a sign we must multiply this by 9: = 90′ = 1°30′ Gemini. Similarly the Moon at 16 Taurus 42 has just entered a Gemini sector. In this case it is 2′ into the sector: 2′ X 9 =18′ Gemini, i.e. 0°18′ Gemini, so that the Sun and Moon will appear in fairly close conjunction in the Navamsa chart.

A moment's reflection will reveal that what the Navamsa chart is doing is to bring out all the 40°—based aspects in a radical chart showing them as conjunctions, all 20°—based aspects as oppositions and so on. In other words the Navamsa chart is not just related to the concept of harmonics, it is in fact the ninth harmonic chart pure and simple!

By dividing each sign by nine and then allocating the resultant segments to the 12 signs from 0° Aries the original twelve-fold division of the circle disappears and is replaced by a ninefold division.

It will be found that, provided the resultant segments are grouped into twelves it will always hold good that to divide a sign by any number is to divide the circle by that number. This is important for it would in fact seem more than likely that the practice of referring to Shodasavargas as divisions of the signs is in fact erroneous and that these were originally understood as divisions of the circle (5). Since the result is the same this may seem irrelevant. However, if these divisions refer directly to the circle it indicates that their conception was independent of the number 12 with which we in the west have become obsessed to our great disadvantage (6). The 12-sign zodiac in this context is being used both for the measurement of the phase angle of a body within any particular cycle, i.e., as a measuring circle, and as an interpretative basis in terms of planetary rulerships (7).

What we mean by the Navamsa chart being the ninth harmonic chart may be more clearly understood if we look again more closely at the derivation of the Navamsa chart. To obtain the chart the positions of the radical chart are translated in the manner described above and are then transcribed on to a *single* zodiac. Now, though we transcribe these positions on to a second diagram we must not forget that the positions of the planets have not in fact moved at all. What has happened is that we have introduced a nine-fold wave into the circle and then condensed all nine waves into one wave by superimposition. What appear in the *single*

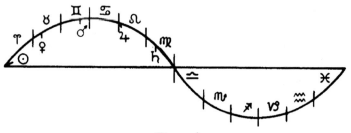

Figure 1
The Single Cycle of 360° in Its 12 Signs Form

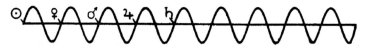

Figure 2
The Ninefold Wave from which the Navamsa is Condensed by Super Imposition. (The bodies shown would all be placed at 0 Aries)

Navamsa chart as conjunctions, oppositions and so on, are in fact expressions of the relative phasing of the individual factors on these *nine* waves. A conjunction in the Navamsa indicates that the two bodies in question are in phase on this harmonic; an opposition that these bodies are 180° out of phase. And this is of course quite independent of which of the nine waves the factors are on.

If in a radical chart the Sun were at 0° Aries, Venus at 10° Taurus, Mars at 20° Gemini, Jupiter at 0° Leo, Saturn at 10° Virgo, these would all appear in 0° Aries in the Navamsa chart as will be seen in figures 1 and 2.

Some consideration of the traditional interpretation of the Navamsa chart will be given in Part II. However it may be noted here that the main emphasis in interpretation is upon aspectual relationships within the Navamsa chart. It will be seen from the above diagram that aspectual relationships refer to the relative phasing within different cycles. For example the factor which would appear to confer power to a conjunction in the Navamsa chart is that all the bodies in question are at the same stage, i.e., phase, in their respective cycles.

While the Navamsa chart is by far the most popular in Hindu astrology the other Vargas (divisions) are by no means neglected. Their calculation is for the most part along the same lines as for the Navamsa, though there do appear to be certain anomalies (7). The 6, 7 and 16 divisions appear to be equally straightforward harmonic charts while the allocation of rulerships in some of the other divisions is slightly less clear-cut, the rulerships being given in terms of planets rather than signs. Two separate concepts would appear to have been confused at this point and it is hoped to consider them later on.

The discovery of the idea of harmonics in Hindu astrology under a different guise opens up an enormous new field for research which could bring Hindu and western astrology together into an extremely fruitful relationship. Some idea of the possible wealth of material that this traditional form of harmonics may hold was further emphasized by the recent arrival of a fascinating booklet *The Golden Key to Rectify Birth Time* (8). The methods outlined in this booklet are based on what purports to be a specific rhythmic ebb and flow of possible birth moments throughout the day. This ebb and flow, it is purported, is regulated by the interaction of the positions of the Sun, Moon, Ascendant and Moon's Nodes with their positions as translated into a chart calculated from the twelfth division of the twelfth division of a sign: the so-called Prana Dwadasamsa chart. Here we are entering the field of micro-harmonics. A movement of 5″ (seconds) of arc in the radical chart is equivalent to 2°24′ of arc in the Prana Dwadasamsa chart, or 10′ of arc in the radical equates to nine signs 18°00′ in this chart! Whatever the truth of this method of rectification, and it most certainly deserves a full investigation, it is eloquent testimony as to the enormous depth of what we would call harmonic analysis, that the Hindus have already applied in their study of the individual birth chart.

References and Notes

1. *The Astrological Magazine*, monthly, edited by B. V. Raman, Raman Publications, Bangalore.

2. Raman, B. V., *Varshaphal or the Hindu Progressed Horoscope*, p.31.

3. Winyard, C. A. "The Hidden Strength in Your chart," *The Astrological Journal*, Vol. I, No. 3, pp. 15-17 and additional tables. See also: Fagan, Cyril, "The Novien." *Spica*, Vol. VIII, No. 2, pp. 13-19 where the idea of the Navamsa as an aspectarian-vernier for measuring micro-aspects is discussed.

4. Raman, B. V. *A Manual of Hindu Astrology*. First edition, p. 90.

5. Op. cit. pp. 95-96, Art. 119 dealing with the Navamsa refers to its origin having been formulated in view of the relationship between degrees of the ecliptic and the stellar points or Nakshatras, i.e., constellations. The Nakshatras are 27 in number. Therefore each Nakshatra gets 13⅓°. Each Nakshatra is further subdivided into four padas, quarters, so that one pada is 3⅓° of the ecliptic arc. The author then goes on to say, "Similarly a sign is divided into nine equal parts and each is a Navamsa. The Bhachakra, zodiac, is divided into 108 Navamsas and each Navamsa corresponds to a Nakshatra Pada," (i.e., a quarter constellation). Here and elsewhere there is evidence of considerable ambiguity and confusion as to the origin of the divisions.

6. Addey, J. M. "Seven-thousand Doctors," *The Astrological Journal*, Vol. XI, No. 4, Autumn 1969, p. 20.

7. Hindu astrology places enormous value on the rulers of the signs and a great part of the evaluation of these secondary charts stresses the rulerships of the divisions in which a planet is found, and for some divisions a sequence of planetary rulerships is given rather than of signs. Certain planets and certain divisions would seem to have a specific affinity and planets become highly potent by occupying certain kinds of divisions, owned by them, or by planets declared as their intimate friends or by such divisions being their

own places of exaltation or fall. (*A Manual of Hindu Astrology*, Art. 105). A full exploration of these relationships may bring to light specific affinities between certain harmonics and certain planets, and may provide a rationale for exaltations and other degrees on harmonic lines.

8. *The Golden Key to Rectify Birth Time* by V. Govindapillai, Kalapavanam Press, Point Pedro, 1969.

9. *The Key to Determine the Span of Life* by V. Govindapillai, Kalapavanam Press, Point Pedro, 1967, p. 29 refers to the radical chart as representing the physical body and compared it to a tree, while the Navamsa chart is compared to its fruits and is referred to as representing the soul of the native.

Chapter 10

Five-fold Divisions and Subdivisions in Astrology

So far the emphasis in the study of the harmonic basis of astrology had been almost entirely on the mechanics of the theory; this was necessary in order to show that astrological laws really did conform to harmonic patterns.

There was a danger that people would begin to think that the whole study was a matter of dry statistics. It was therefore necessary to begin to develop the study of number symbolism in relation to harmonics so as to show that we really were moving towards a greater interpretative potential.

J.M.A., 1976

* * *

It seems of vital importance to the understanding of the ideas I have, for some time, been putting forward, that the inner, qualitative side of the picture (which was always present and to which I have drawn attention from time to time) should be more explicitly developed, lest the real nature and purpose of the work be lost sight of or misconstrued.

It will be appreciated that my criticism of present-day astrology is that it is fragmented, partitive and lacking those principles which will give the subject a real unity, that is a unity which provides for all the potentialities of the subject and offers a truly comprehensive basis for every aspect of interpretative symbolism.

We may call the astrology which *does* provide such a basis, integral astrology, that is an astrology which is whole and complete, possessing all necessary and appropriate parts. It is towards such an astrology (far-distant as we are from it) that we should be trying to move.

The picture which is now emerging from the reduction of astrological symbolism to its simplest elements is of a remarkable code based upon the rhythms of cosmic cycles (that is upon the harmonics of cosmic periods), wonderfully simple in its essence, exceedingly complex in its manifestation, capable of infinite adaptation and flexibility in its application. It appears to be the source of all the traditional doctrines which have come down to us from the past and of all new concepts which emerge from time to time in the present.

The decipherment of this code depends upon an understanding of the symbolism of cosmic existences, upon a mastery of the symbolism of ideal numbers and of the right relation of both to the life of man and nature.

It is a formidable task but in attempting its solution we have at our disposal three types of tool, each of immense scope and power.

The first is inductive scientific method and reasoning by which conclusions are drawn and hypotheses built up and tested from a study of the world about us. One example of such a tentative conclusion is given later.

The second avenue of approach is via the study of tradition, for it is clear that the ancient traditions of astrology (now largely lost or stripped down to a handful of simple rules) contained, in their purity, a most profound and comprehensive system of symbolism. An example of the scrutiny of tradition to see what it has to tell us about our present problems, is afforded by Charles Harvey's study of Hindu astrology (which has preserved a far more diverse tradition than current western astrology).

The third tool at our disposal is that of deductive philosophic reasoning from first principles. It is easy to see how each of these three modes of approach steadies, supplements and fortifies the other two. This article is intended to exemplify the third type of approach.

Those who have read Charles Harvey's article will probably have grasped the concept of the division of the complete circle of the horoscope into subordinate circles or cycles—in the case of the Navamsa chart, into nine subordinate cycles.

Now the nine waves of the ninth harmonic are simply nine cycles or circles within the full circle; a wave is only a circle somewhat straightened out and in fixing the positions of planets in the Navamsa chart we are simply fixing their position in the ninth harmonic. All this is explained in Charles Harvey's article.

The horoscope, it transpires (and this lies behind all the subdivisions of Hindu astrology) is constructed along the same lines as that little gas or electric meter which we all have at home in the cellar or under the stairs. There is one dial for units, one for tens, one for hundreds, one for thousands and so on. *And each dial deals with the measurements which are appropriate to it, and with those only.*

Now in recent years a good deal has been heard of the 90°-dial introduced by the Ebertin School. In using this instrument the planetary positions of the horoscope are transposed from the full circle of 360° and given new positions showing their relationship to the 90°-sector in which they are situated, each 90°-sector being reexpressed as a full cycle or circle in its own right.

The effect of this is to highlight the relationship of planets to each other in the fourth harmonic, and since the number four is so important in relation to the idea of *manifestation*, the relationships revealed by the 90°-dial are found, by those who use them, to be very significant.

The criticism might be made however, that the twelve-fold structure of the zodiac is *already adapted* to reveal, to the eye of the experienced astrologer, relationships within the 90°-sector. A thorough grasp of the triplicities enables him to spot most of these without the help of a dial.

But it is now clear from the harmonic analyses of horoscopic factors which have been done that, if we are to restore to astrology its integral character, we must learn to understand clearly the symbolism of all numbers and to read aright the measurements shown on many other dials besides the 90°-dial.

The great importance of the twelve-fold division of the zodiac arises simply because it can be divided by one, two, three, four and six, and thus is adapted to *incorporate the symbolism* of all these numbers. But what of the division by five, seven, eight and nine?

The symbolism of the twelve signs has been explored and written about again and again until it has soaked into us and become part of our very thinking. We must now set ourselves to explore and to become just as thoroughly familiar with the symbolism of other numbers so that we know exactly what order of classification they deal with.

This article (after a rather long-winded start) deals with the first of these neglected but profoundly important numbers: five.

There are, in a broad sense, I believe, two principal ways in which the symbolism of a number can be considered: the first is from its place in the procession from unity (and especially its place in the first nine numbers) and the second is through a study of the composition of the number. These two main viewpoints and the various aspects of them, as when five is seen as the combination of two and three or of one and four, are merely different ways of looking at one reality. Thomas Taylor speaks of the Pentad[10] as "uniting the first two differing species of number, the odd and the even, (i.e., 2 and 3) becoming itself the system of their association."

What then is this system which unites the duad and the triad? There are a number of ways, but since we are interested in the application of five to the human nativity it will be best to find out how this system applies to man's life in the realms of manifestation.

Now although man is spirit, soul and body, yet the incarnating unity of his *manifested* life is the soul and when we view man from below we see soul as the primal unity (subject) with body as its outward vehicle and expression (object). This constitutes our basic duad: soul above and body below. The triad is formed by the three classes of soul faculty: mind, will and heart (which address themselves to the true, the good and the beautiful respectively).

Thus we have a trinity of faculties united above in soul and below in body.

SOUL

HEART   WILL   MIND

BODY

This is, so to speak, the human pentad in the manifested order which we shall see clearly expressed over and over again in man's outward life and institutions and, indeed, in his very body. We shall always find them arranged in the same descending order: soul—mind—will—heart—body.

General Correlations

First, in order to be clear about the basic character of each of these principles, let us outline the function of each in human life.

_____

[10] *The Theoretic Arithmetic of the Pythagoreans* (Thos Taylor) Book III.

Under the heading of mind are included all man's gnostic powers, from the highest to the lowest; all the means by which he achieves knowledge and understanding. These, we shall see, are capable of a five-fold classification. In the larger sphere of man's terrestrial life they express themselves in human PHILOSOPHY and SCIENCE; in fact in man's search for truth.

Under "will" are included all man's elective and purposive faculties, all the graduations and faculty by which he makes and adheres to a choice between good and evil, or more properly, between a greater and a lesser good. These also are capable of a five-fold division and find their larger expression in man's RELIGION, that is, in his active life in conformity with ideals and principles.

Under "heart" are included every aspect of man's affectional and aspirational nature, that is every faculty through which he admires the beautiful or delightful, gives his allegiance to it and seeks to enjoy and express it. These also are capable of a five-fold division and express themselves, in the larger sense, in man's ART.

Under "body" is included not only man's physical and other bodies but also, in a sense, all man's contact with the mundane order and his work, turning downwards and outwards, in building the City of God on earth.

"Soul" represents the unification of man's faculties as they turn upwards and inwards in the quest to know, love and unite with God. Among human activities it correlates with MYSTICISM.

Mind: The Gnostic Powers

There are five branches of these corresponding to the five-fold order already described. They are: intuition, reason, opinion, instinct and sense. Intuition, like *soul*, is unitive in relation to the other four; reason is the most characteristically human mental faculty corresponding in our original pentad to mind; the third faculty, which I have called opinion, might equally well be called judgment or estimation. (This faculty is above instinct but below reason: if we are asked how far it is to the post office we do not refer the problem to the instincts, yet, although we deliberate briefly, we do not refer it to the reason proper). This gnostic faculty correlates with will because it is the one which most characteristically precedes action in our everyday lives.

The two lower gnostic faculties, instinct and sense, are self-evident. The former corresponds to *heart* because it informs us of those things in which the natural desires and appetencies are the governing factors.

Each of these five branches of the gnostic powers divide again naturally into five sub-branches. The five senses (body) are the most obvious and are dealt with below. To enumerate all the sub-branches of the others might seem pedantic but each subdivision of the gnostic faculties has its characteristic objects of knowledge.

Will: The Conscience

The function of the will is to control. It is galvanized by the heart and guided by the head, but it has the special quality of fixity so that it can hold to a certain course when the impulse from the heart which originally moved it and the illumination from the mind which originally directed it, are no longer present.

Ideally the will puts and holds all things in their proper places and relationships. That is to say it ordinates and coordinates.

Closely associated with will is the concept of conscience. It is sometimes assumed that the conscience is simple and of one nature but in fact we can see, on closer inspection, that it has a five-fold composition in conformity to the principles already laid down.

Crudely put, conscience chooses between good and bad. We can then see that at the level of what is good or bad for the body there is a moral instinct; at the level of heart a moral sentiment, at the level of will a moral habit and above that a moral reason and a moral intuition.

A man may, for example, have a conscientious objection to military service. But what lies behind this objection may vary qualitatively. At the lowest level his instincts may have told him that a soldier's life will involve him in dangers which he does not care for; or he may be guided by sentiment (like Arjuna, in his famous dialogue with Krishna in the *Bhagavadgita*, when he pleaded that many of those arrayed against him were his own kindred and friends). Or he may have been brought up as a Quaker or in some other sect with strong teachings against military service, and if he is to stand by the religious principles of his upbringing he will refuse to enlist.

So far (and without anticipating his ultimate decision) we can see that he has not used the right faculty for the job; only the moral reason or moral intuition (which will never conflict with the reason, even though it reach its conclusion by a shorter route) can decide the right or wrong of such a matter. But that is not to say that there are not certain matters where the moral instinct, say, is not the most appropriate faculty for the job.

The Heart

Just in the same way that we have found five branches of the gnostic and volitional powers, so we can make the same distinction in relation to the affectional and aesthetic faculties. This is not difficult and the reader may try it for himself.

The Arts of Mankind

We have suggested that in terms of the broad picture of human activity, the will corresponds to religion. Again we can see that the religions of mankind could be grouped via our classification according to whether they were essentially mystical (soul) or cultivated primarily the ideals of truth and understanding (mind) or morality (will) or devotion (heart) or various kinds of phenomenalism, such as spiritism (body).

Similarly the arts of mankind have been correlated with heart.

Now, although we usually associate art with what are called the fine arts because they are especially concerned with the realization and expression of beauty, yet, in the wider sense, all human activities may be regarded as arts. Thus we have the art of the physician, the teacher or the welder.

In this way all human activities can be classified according to our five-fold order. Highest are those activities which subserve the art of the perfect life; these correspond to soul and represent the unification and blending of all subordinate powers in the realization and service of the ideal.

Then come those arts—they are primarily of a teaching character in the widest sense—which have as their object the unfoldment of Truth in the mind. Next come those arts which play an ordinative role in society, just as the will does in the life of the individual. Medicine, politics, the services, law, the church (what we usually call the professions) are, for example, of this nature.

Below this are those arts which are connected with the realization of the beautiful and enjoyable in life. These correlate with heart and include all the so-called fine arts, the arts of the entertainer and so on.

At the bottom of the scale, corresponding to body, are those arts which are of a purely pragmatic nature, usefully meeting all the thousand and one practical needs in man's life.

It is easy to see that each of these divisions will divide and subdivide again and again by five. Thus in my article on the Sun positions of physicians (one of the five branches of the ordinative arts) in the *Journal*, I mention that Paracelsus speaks of the five sects of physicians who specialize in the five types of bodily disorder.

The Caste System

Now it is obvious that although it is possible to make a theoretical five-fold division of human activities along these lines, according to their dominant purpose and intention, yet in practice it is of course very difficult and this is confirmed by the somewhat tangled multiplicity of orders into which the Indian caste system (which was and is clearly based on our classification in its purity) has split up in practice.

However, we can still see the framework quite clearly: four traditional castes carrying on the activities listed in the previous section and united by a fifth group which is above them all. The highest caste is that of the Brahmans (mind), then the Kshatriyas (military and governing, corresponding to will), the Vaishyas (trading and agricultural which correspond to heart in this system because they directly minister to man's needs as a living being) and the Sudras (mental and artisan).

But over and above these four groups there is, in effect a fifth group of those who have turned away from the world and all that these four castes stand for in the way of separate interests. These are of course the holy men who have chosen to devote themselves to God, and into this group men from any other caste group may pass; thus it unites the other four.

Types of Government

In the *Republic* of Plato a picture is drawn of an ideal state and its government. It is essentially a state in which all factors and forces have been co-ordinated so that a condition of unity and harmony prevails. Thus, in terms of a political ideal it represents the first and highest of our five categories.

By the time the eighth book is reached the character of this republic has been fully described but Socrates agrees that in the realms of change such a state cannot survive and then he goes on to describe, in response to questions, *the four successive stages of government* down the scale of which events are likely to slide when the ideal republic ceases to prevail.

He says that such different types of states do not grow on trees ("are not gathered from the rocks" is his phrase, I think) but arise because they correspond to the type of men who live in them. I will not spoil the fun for those who have not read this chapter but will only say that the next-to-last type of government is a democracy and it corresponds to heart in our classification. Those who like their bed-time reading to be a bit spine-chilling could do worse than read Socrates' description of a democracy. They will have no difficulty in recognizing the whole swinging scene (one in which everybody does just whatever he has a fancy to do).

Socrates shows that each type of government is overthrown by the *thing it prizes most*—in the case of a democracy, freedom. So the people choose for themselves a champion who will free them from some supposed oppression—only to find themselves landed with the lowest class of government, a tyranny.

The Hand

In our last two examples the emphasis in our five has been upon *four* subordinated to *one* superior and unifying principle.

If we wish to see a living embodiment of this aspect of the pentad, we have only to lift up our hand, juxtapose the thumb in front of the four fingers and let the tips of our fingers bend over to gather about the head of the thumb.

The symbolism of the thumb as representing man's status as a self-conscious rational being (which necessarily implies an individual soul) is well known, and the other fingers are arranged in the now-familiar order: the index or teaching finger (mind), the middle or Saturn finger (will), the Sun or Apollo finger (heart) and the little finger, Mercury in its Virgo aspect, (body).

An appreciation and recollection of this arrangement enables one to understand much about the symbolism of the hand and its movements.

The Nadiamsas

I believe the principal (or at least one important) manifestation of the five-fold classification in Indian astrology are the nadiamsas.

The nadis are one-fifth part of a degree (12′)—150 to a sign—divided into a positive and negative

half (one is really dealing with the 1,800th harmonic) and the literature of Indian astrology contains descriptions, for each nadi, of the native's life (based, I think, on the Moon's position), giving the place and conditions of birth and parentage, caste, vocation, marriage, children, length of life and so on.

It will be appreciated that the smaller the division, the more distinctions it incorporates. Thus, if we divide the horoscope m two, east and west, it will only tell us of self and not-self. If we divide it again, north and south, we shall have four quadrants each with its characteristics; if we superimpose on this the division by three we have 12 divisions each capable of telling us about a considerable variety of things (but quite useless for telling us about other things). So, as one goes on dividing and subdividing the circle, the segments come to include an ever greater range of distinctions.

In considering the basic character given to our five-fold nadi division we see two things: first that it is based on precisely the same model we have been dealing with but, second, that while the principles dealt with are, in their purity, the same, the planetary symbols used may not at first seem apt.

The five nadis of each degree are ruled successively (Mr. Abayacoon tells me) by Mars-fire (will), Saturn-air (mind) Jupiter-ether (soul), Mercury-earth (body) and Venus- water (heart).

When the two ends of this cycle are joined up the order is, of course, the same as in our other examples, but it will be seen that whilst Mercury still represents earth and body (as in the digits of .the hand) Venus has taken the place of Sun as the symbol for heart. This is a perfectly acceptable change. Some will query Saturn for air (mind) but this, too, has perfectly respectable symbolic antecedents: Milton's poem, *Il Penseroso*, describes a perfect Saturn type: the sober, thoughtful, introspective philosophical man. And so on.

This is an exercise in looking past the planetary symbol to see how and in what sense it is used.

The Five Senses

We saw earlier that one of the five branches of the gnostic faculties was sense—or, as we usually say, the senses. Being now experienced in the use of our five-fold classification we shall have no difficulty in allocating each of the five senses to its place in this system.

Touch, being dependent upon physical contact, goes with *body*; taste being connected with what we enjoy (as when we say something is to our taste) and the word being, furthermore, employed as expressive of aesthetic appreciation and judgment, goes with *heart*; sight clearly goes with *mind* for we constantly use such metaphors as "I see," "to throw light on," which connect vision with understanding; hearing and sound are connected with will as when we think of the word or logos as expressive of God's will—that which has been uttered or ordained. This leaves us with smell, the most elusive, unitive and evocative of the senses as correlated with soul and the mystical element in life.

This allocation (like all the others, indeed) is profoundly interesting. Smell, like the intuition, gives a unitive impression as when, in certain circumstances, we may speak of the smell of evil, the odor of sanctity, the perfume-of prayer or holiness, the fragrance of memory. But all these allocations are deeply informative.

Five-fold Divisions in the Horoscope

So far we have been gaining experience and practice in understanding and applying our five-fold classification in different fields, but we have not yet attempted to apply these distinctions to the horoscope. This, however, should be our ultimate purpose and it is obvious that the five senses provide us with a good field in which to test our knowledge.

(The third house, for example, will often tell us of a defect in the senses, but this is only because it deals with our communicative appetancy and our knowledge of relationships and a defect in one of the senses is an impediment in this field. But the third house does not *distinguish* between the senses—how could it?)

At the time when material for this article was being assembled, my wife remarked one day that the piano needed tuning and it crossed my mind that I was slightly acquainted with a blind piano-tuner who, if his time of birth were known, might provide the ideal subject for a study of the senses since, in his case, the loss of one sense had been matched by the enhancement of another. My best expectations were exceeded for, being unmarried and having lived with his mother until her death, he was able to state definitely that he was born towards midnight, that it was after 11:30 and before 11:45 p.m. and he suggested that 11:40 p.m. on January 4, 1906 (S. London) would almost certainly be within five minutes of the correct time. This gives us our horoscope (figure 1).

The native states that he became blind on his tenth birthday as a result of cerebro-spinal meningitis. A most interesting person, he combines the affable and courteous demeanor of Libra rising with the resolute independence of ruler conjunction Uranus. He travels freely on his own about London on public transport and, apart from the special development of the hearing faculty needed by a piano tuner, he appears to be a most fluent and sensitive pianist.

148

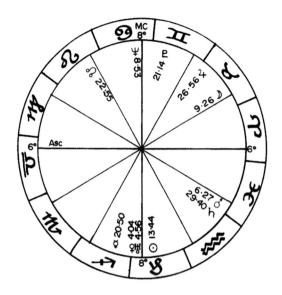

Figure 1

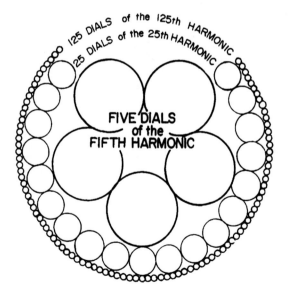

Figure 2

Now those readers who recall what was said at the beginning of this article about the horoscope as a system of dials and who have related this to the five-fold system of symbolism since described, will have realized that it is suggested that, as we divide and subdivide human nature, its qualities, faculties and attributes into successive divisions of five, we are really moving down through the successive divisions of the 5th harmonic, that is through the 5th, the 25h (5 X 5), the 125th (5 X 5 X 5) and so on and that, if we are going to look for some abnormality in one of these five-fold divisions of man, then we shall find it in one place *and one place only*, namely in one of these five-fold divisions in the horoscope.

The position can be represented diagrammatically as in figure 2: each of the five waves of the 5th harmonic is like a cycle or circle; each one a little zodiac; the same applies to the 25th and the 125th.

One has to discover the position of the planets in these minor cycles, putting all the positions in the 5th harmonic of 72° *into one circle* (just as all the positions in each 90° are put into one circle in the case of the 90° dial) and so on with each lesser harmonic.

Now in the case of the 5th harmonic of five 72° waves it is easy to work out the new positions. If there are 72° to a full circle then each sign will be 6° in extent and a planet in, say, 9° Aries will be in 15° Taurus in the new circle. But the 25th harmonic (with a wavelength of 14° 24′) is very difficult and the 125th, where the whole cycle of 12 signs is compressed into 2°52.8′ is worse.

Now at present we are feeling our way in this field but if our theory is correct a chart such as the one given should show indications of blindness when transferred to one of these five-fold charts. Perhaps it will show in more than one; perhaps actual physical blindness does not appear unless there is something which corresponds to this at every level.

This article is already a long one so I must leave those who are interested to work out the new positions for themselves—this will be useful practice before starting to experiment with your own chart—but those who work out the new positions will find that this chart, when transposed to the 5th harmonic has:

Mercury 14.10 Scorpio, Neptune 14.25 Leo and Pluto 16.10 Taurus. This gives a very close and very characteristic T-cross. Mercury opposition Pluto and square Neptune.

In the 25th harmonic: Mercury 10.50 Taurus, Neptune 11.40 Aquarius and Mars 11.15 Leo, an almost exact and very typical T-cross.

In the 125th harmonic: Mercury 24.10 Libra, Mars 26.15 Capricorn and Neptune 0.25 Leo, another close and typical T-cross.

Each of these is independent of the other.

Notice that in the 25th harmonic an orb of 1' in the natal map becomes an orb of 25', and in the 125th harmonic a natal orb of 1' becomes 125' (or 2°05').

What does this mean in terms of our T-crosses? There are six aspects involved, four squares, two oppositions. It will now be seen that, of these six, three show an orb in the *natal* map of 1', two show an orb of 2' and the sixth 3'. Thus the relationship of the planets in these T-crosses is fully appropriate as to meaning, almost exact in closeness and totally invisible from an ordinary examination of the natal map.

The one thing which cannot yet be pinpointed, *but the possibility of which seems to me to be fully implicit in the result*, is exactly how to distinguish blindness from, say, deafness by die subdivisions of the ecliptic occupied by planets.

I said in the introductory part of this article that I would give an example of an inductive conclusion from this field of study. The

T-cross abovementioned in the 25th harmonic is extremely apt; not only does Mercury fall in the third house of the new map (that based on the new Ascendant) but its square to Mars in Leo in the sixth looks very characteristic of cerebro-spinal meningitis.

Now it will be appreciated that squares in the 25th harmonic, if they are to be reduced to their simplest expression, can be regarded as conjunctions in the 100th harmonic (4 X 25).

This is interesting because, thanks to the good offices of Axel Harvey, a massive program of harmonic analysis by computer has recently been undertaken comprising over 20,000 sets of birth data and from all these data *the most outstanding single result was the 100th harmonic in the Sun position of sufferers from paralytic poliomyelitis.*

We therefore have two outstanding results which seem to link extreme injury to the nervous system with the 100th harmonic.

There are a great many other things that could be said about this example, and as to the number five, one has only scratched the surface of its symbolism.

I am particularly sorry that there is no room to write about the very important aspect of the symbolism of this number which derives from its central position in the first nine numbers (which according to the Pythagoreans were the only numbers):

$$
\begin{array}{ccc}
1 & 2 & 3 \\
4 & 5 & 6 \\
7 & 8 & 9
\end{array}
$$

The great importance of this station of the number five, which puts it, like man himself, at the cross-roads of all forces, is fraught with great interest but we must leave that for another occasion.

Chapter 11

The Maps of Delinquents

The contribution to the winter issue of *Spica* (1970) by Ivon Hyde, in which he draws attention to the very unusual distribution of the Sun in the nativities of 391 delinquent children, is of exceptional interest and I should be grateful for an opportunity to comment upon his findings.

There is one exceptional feature of the graph which he gives to show the solar distribution in the zodiac: *that is the huge totals which are thrown up in the first decanates of Aries and Libra.*

For some years I have been expounding a new view of the basis of astrological effects. This postulates that all astrological effects are based in the *harmonics of cosmic periods.*

This is not an easy doctrine to understand (although it becomes very much easier when one actually works with it) and I think it may help students to see certain points if I showed how this approach would explain Ivon Hyde's results.

We are dealing with delinquent children. What makes a child delinquent? Surely their delinquency arises because they possess a certain combination of characteristic qualities that puts them in disharmony with the society in which they live.

Perhaps in another society this very combination of characteristics would qualify them for admiration rather than disapproval; perhaps not. The point is that it is because they have a certain *combination* of qualities that they are evidently at war with their environment.

Now if we are dealing with a *combination* of qualities we must look at our results in such a way as to see in them different factors actually combining to give the unusual feature observed (in this case the peak in the first decanates of Aries and Libra).

Now I maintain that the view which modern research is leading us to accept, postulates that the different qualities in the horoscope are shown by dividing the cosmic cycles by different numbers and observing the rhythms based in these different numerical divisions.

In this case the cosmic cycle we are dealing with is the yearly (solar) cycle. That is to say we are observing the position of the Sun in its annual passage through the zodiac.

Now in this cycle we are accustomed to think first and foremost of the 12 signs of the zodiac—but perhaps we are asking too much of these 12 overworked divisions. Evidently we are, for, as Ivon Hyde points out, the unusual features of his results *would not show up* if he had given the totals for the 12 signs; it is only when we look at the 36 decanates that we see the significant element in the figures.

Ivon Hyde says he was tempted, in an effort to find the significant divisions of the ecliptic which gave this result, to consider some of the Indian divisions such as the Navamsa. But the Indians use many, many divisions and there is no special reason why we should chose the Navamsa which, after all, is in itself too small to give a high total for a whole decanate.

The scientific solution is to consider all possible divisions.

This is the function of harmonic analysis (or, Fourier Analysis, as it is sometimes called) which, in effect, considers the part

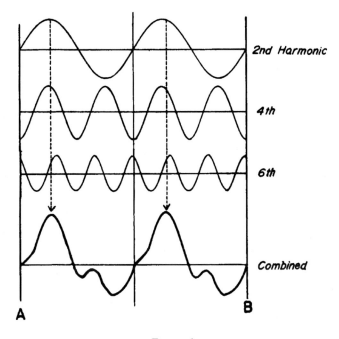

2nd Harmonic

4th

6th

Combined

A   B

Figure 1

played by every possible division of the cycle involved. The problem is to break down a distribution pattern, such as Ivon Hyde has
given us, into its constituent rhythms.

Now there is one rule of the utmost importance and of univer-
sal applicability to give results of this kind. It can be stated thus:

*If a high-scoring area in one half of the zodiac is matched by
an outstanding low-scoring area at the opposite point, then the
distribution is dominated by the odd-numbered harmonics.*

We will draw three even numbered harmonics and then show
how they combine. Figure 1 shows a) the second, b) the fourth, c)
the sixth harmonics of the period AB and d) the way in which these
three waves combine.

We see that the result of combining the three even-numbered harmonics is to throw up a "high" at exactly the same place in each half because the pattern is repeated in each half of the series. If the period AB represents one complete circle then a peak in one half of the zodiac will be matched by a peak at exactly the opposite point.

Now, since by far the best way, (in fact the only way I believe), to learn about wave complexes is to start drawing them out, I suggest that the reader gets pencil and paper and tries out the effect of first drawing and then combining, three *odd numbered* harmonics (having, say, one wave, three waves, and five waves).

Make the peaks of the three wave series coincide at one point in the first half as we have done in figure 1, and see what happens at the corresponding point in the second *half*.

To return now to Ivon Hyde's results we can see that his graph, having a peak in the first half of the zodiac exactly matched by a peak at the opposite point comes in the category of *wave complexes, which are dominated by even-numbered harmonics*.

In figure 2, I have drawn out, in graph form, a) the totals for the *first six signs* in the Sun positions of his delinquents, b) the totals for the second six signs and c) the combined totals for the two halves put together, so that it shows the typical 180° distribution.

Now a mathematician could subject Mr. Hyde's totals to harmonic analysis so as to be able to say exactly what harmonics are present in his distribution and in what proportion. I have not done this, but from long experience of looking at combinations of wave forms I can estimate approximately what combination of harmonics would give a result which would describe Mr. Hyde's distribution pattern.

The harmonics involved will be characteristically even-numbered and the waves will coincide at two places (and two places only), that is, of course, at the beginning of Aries and Libra.

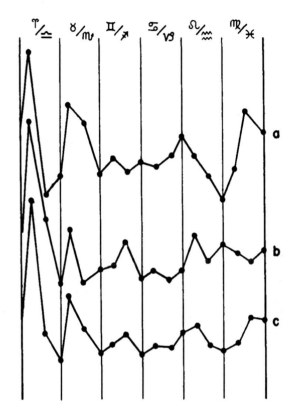

Figure 2
Distribution of Delinquents' Suns—a, First Six Signs; b, Second Six
Signs; c, First and Second Six Signs Combined (see figure 3)

I would suggest that the 12th harmonic (12 waves of 30°), the 10th (10 waves of 36°), the 6th (6 waves of 60°) and the 2nd (two of 180°) would approximately describe the distribution pattern.

One needs to draw out only half of each wave series, since the *second half exactly repeats the first.*

Figure 3 draws out the four harmonics I suggest, and combines them. This combined wave complex is then compared with

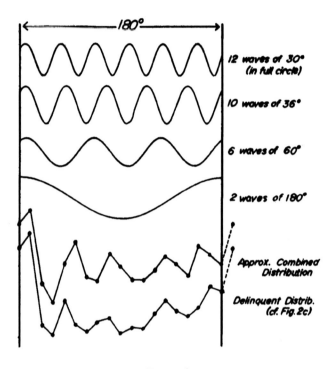

Figure 3

figure 2c (the 180° Sun distribution pattern in Mr. Hyde's delinquents).

The match is not an exact but this is because I have done the job roughly and by estimate. It is probable that there is at least one other strong harmonic involved (say the 20th; 20 waves of 18°) which would push up the peak at the beginning.

Anyone who thinks over the implication of the foregoing and preferably draws out the results for himself on squared paper will, I believe, be a step nearer answering Mr. Hyde's question as to what makes astrology tick.

Chapter 12

The Unity of Harmonics, Aspects, Antiscions, Midpoints and Other Mean Points

Students may well wonder if there is not a general formula covering the apparently capricious variety of configurations in astrology—aspects, antiscions, midpoints and others. That such a general formula exists is mathematically trivial but now widely known, so I am stating here: a planet at longitude Po is configured by one or more planets at P1 , P2, . . . , Pn if the identity

$$\pm (P_1 + P_2 + \ldots P_n)/n = P_o + 2\pi j/kn$$

is true, where j is any integer and k any integer except zero. At least three special cases of this formula are quite familiar.

1. With n = 1 and the left-hand expression positive. This yields the aspects: j = k or j = 0, conjunctions; j nonzero and k = 2, oppositions; k = 3, trines; and so forth. Of course these aspects are also harmonic relationships. Thus if k= 125, the two points configure one another in the 125th harmonic.

2. With n = 1 and the left-hand expression negative. If j = 0 or k = 1 this gives us the traditional antiscion (two planets equidistant from an equinoctial point—the terminology varies).

3. With n = 2 and the left-hand expression positive. This is the midpoint or, as the Germans aptly call it, the half-sum. In the Ebertin system, k has been set arbitrarily or empirically at 4, since only multiples of 45° are thought to be valid aspects for midpoints; however, I doubt that the last word has been said.

4. With n greater than 2. I call this configuration the mean point: it is n longitudes added together and divided by n, the mid-point being a special case of it.

The mean point brings us to configurations which, while they are covered by the general formula, have not received much attention from astrologers. Interested readers may investigate these for themselves but I shall mention four matters for their benefit. First, the smallest number of mean points one can assign to any n planets; second, the antiscion of order k and its relationship to harmonics; third, how antiscions depend on the choice of a fiducial; fourth, notation.

What is the smallest number of mean points for any n planets?

Consider five planets, A, B, C, D, E, at longitudes 0°, 40°, 125°, 170° and 285°, respectively. Now rotate the coordinate system so that each planet in turn occupies the zero degree station. We thus obtain five sets of longitudes.

A	0	320	235	190	75
B	40	0	275	230	115
C	125	85	0	315	200
D	170	130	45	0	245
E	285	245	160	115	0
Sum	620	780	715	850	635
M.P.*	124	156	143	170	127
M.P. Red.*	124	196	268	340	52

*M.P.—mean point. M.P.Red.—mean point reduced to the original coordinate system.

When re-transposed to the original coordinate system, the mean points turn out to be evenly spaced around the zodiac. No matter where one places the fiducial from which degrees are counted, the mean point will always be at one or another of these five places. The same is true for any greater or lesser number of planets and, since we have no reason to believe that one mean point somehow has priority over others, it follows that n planets must have at least n mean points; furthermore the mean points are equidistant.

This is already suggested by the general formula, but the foregoing provides a more concrete way of conceiving the idea.

The Antiscion of Order k and Its Relationship to Harmonics

Consider the general formula with $n = 1$, the left-hand expression negative, and j and k of opposite signs. We have

$$- P_1 = P_0 + \Pi j/k$$

or more conveniently

$$P_0 + P_1 = 2 \ \Pi h/k$$

where $h = k - j$.

This is a simple modification of the traditional aspect, with $P_0 + P_1$ replacing $P_0 - P_1$. If $k = 1$ we have the classical antiscion, or antiscion of order 1.

But now let us look at aspects and harmonics—for the sake of simplicity the 12th harmonic with the neatest possible arrangement, namely a wave in phase with the twelve-fold division of the zodiac and with a node or peak at the vernal point (figure 1).

As the example shows, points at four degrees of any sign will

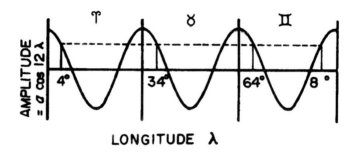

Figure 1

have the same amplitude, which is just another way of saying that they are configured in the 12th harmonic or that they make semisextiles, sextiles, squares, etc., with one another. Now what about the point at 26° of, say, Gemini? Clearly it has the same amplitude as the 4-degree points (positive for a cosine wave, negative for a sine wave). Furthermore it satisfies, with any of these 4-degree points, the identity

$$P_o + P_1 = 2 \Pi h/12$$

I call this configuration an antiscion of order 12.

Thus, stating that P_o and P_1 make an antiscion of order k is equivalent to saying that they have the same amplitude on the wave of the kth harmonic, provided the wave has a peak or node exactly on the fiducial.

Antiscions therefore depend on the choice of a fiducial. As the above considerations show, regular aspects and mid-points are independent of the coordinate system in which longitude is expressed while, on the contrary, antiscions have no meaning—at least in terms of harmonics—unless the fiducial is a nodal or extreme point of the wave in question. This is true not only of antiscions but of all configurations which have a negative left-hand side in the general formula. Perhaps a thorough statisti-

162

cal analysis of these cases will yield some answers to the question of zodiacs "old and new."

Notation. I believe it was Reinhold Ebertin and his German colleagues who introduced the first consistent and versatile system of notation into astrology. With the help of the general formula, we may extend the system so that any configuration can be succinctly expressed. To write down a special case of the identity given at the outset we need to observe (1) whether the left-hand expression is positive or negative, (2) the value of k, and (3) the planets involved in the configuration. The value of j rarely matters.

I suggest keeping the German (international) abbreviations for the planets. The configuring planets can be placed together, their symbols set apart by commas. The configured planet will naturally stand alone. Between one and the other, in parentheses, we can write the value of k; and if the configuration has a negative left-hand side, a minus sign can be included in the parenthesis. Since the value of n is obvious from the number of configuring planets it need not be stated; if n = 1, of course, it does not matter which planet is configured and which is configuring. Here are some examples:

- SO(3)MO. Sun trine Moon.
- SO(6)A. Sun trine, sextile or opposite Ascendant.
- SO,UR(4)M. In Ebertin's system, SO/UR = M. Usually the "=" in German notation indicates a planet at a multiple of 45° from the midpoint, i.e., kn = 4 x 2 = 8.
- MO(1)JU,NE. Moon at the direct midpoint of Jupiter and Neptune.
- MA(-1)JU. Mars and Jupiter in antiscion.
- MA(-12)JU. Mars and Jupiter in antiscion of order 12.
- SO,MO,PL,A,M(1)ME. Mercury at one of the five mean points of Sun, Moon, Pluto, Ascendant and Midheaven.
- SO,MO,PL,A,M(2)ME. Mercury at one of the five above-mentioned points or at a point halfway between two of these.

If more detail is required, we can replace the k between parentheses by j/k. In such cases the configured planet should be written down first and it should be assumed that aspects are measured from this planet in the same direction that ecliptic degrees are counted, that is to say counterclockwise on an ordinary birth man. Thus M(1/10)SA means Saturn 36° east of the Midheaven while M(9/10)SA means Saturn 36° west of the Midheaven.

Mean Points Considered as Midpoints
of Midpoints Ad Infinitum

The case of three planets is particularly elegant. If one takes all possible mid-points of planets situated at a, b, and c, one finds there are three: a,b; b,c; and c,a. If one takes the mid-points of these mid-points, of course there are again three. Now if one continues to take mid-points of mid-points of mid-points (or super-mid-points) a certain number of times, say n, there will always be three resulting super-mid-points, each of which will have a longitude equal to

$$\{A\{[2n -(-1)n]/3+(-1)n\}+b[2n -(-1)n-(-1)n]/3+c[2n -(-1)n]/3\}/2n$$

It is easy enough to show that this longitude, as n becomes very great, approaches

$$(a + b + c)/3$$

In other words, the super-mid-points of three planets approach the mean point as a limit.

Groups of two and three planets are the only ones whose super-mid-points have this kind of stability. With more than three the number of super-mid-points explodes. Thus four planets have six midpoints, fifteen super-mid-points after two operations, 105 super-mid-points after three operations, 5,460 super-mid-points after four operations, and so on. However unlike the super-mid-points of three planets, which approach their mean point as a limit only, the super-mid-points of four planets are often exactly equal to the mean point. An infinite number of operations with four planets will yield an infinite number of values equal to

$$(a + b + c + d)/4.$$

The Fiducial

Since a zodiacal position is an aspect to some agreed fiducial (vernal point or sidereal 0 Aries, as the case may be) the proposed notation can easily be adapted to express relationships between planets in any zodiac, or simply to state the longitude of a planet in one system or another. To accomplish this one need only deal with the vernal point and sidereal fiducial as if they were themselves planets: thus a planet at zero degrees of any sign (tropical) is making a 12th harmonic contact with the vernal point; and so forth. While one might object to such a formalistic way of looking at the two zodiacs, I believe there is an obvious advantage to a language which systematically excludes the notion of a "right" and "wrong" method by taking all fiducials into account.

Chapter 13

Michel Gauquelin
Strikes Again, Part I

Some notes on the four volumes of Series C of
Michel and Francoise Gauquelin's *Psychological
Monographs: Vol. 1 Profession and Heredity* (Re-
sults from Series A and B); *Vol. 2 The Mars Temper-
ament and Sports Champions; Vol. 3 The Saturn
Temperament and Men of Science* and *Vol. 4 the Ju-
piter Temperament and Actors* (Four Vols.: 200
Francs.).

If it should seem that we have not heard so much lately about
the work of Michel Gauquelin, this can only be because good news
travels slowly. In reality he has, with his wife, Francoise, and other
collaborators, been busier than ever, and to remarkable effect. His
two latest volumes *(The Jupiter Temperament*—see above—is not
yet published at the time of writing) describe experiments which
are brilliant in conception, magnificent in execution and mighty
blows for the vindication and reconstruction of astrology, to say
nothing of their contribution to world science which the world will
wake up to in due course.

Besides finding time to carry through his huge program of experiments and write numerous books and articles, Gauquelin has,
step by step, published all his data, full descriptions of his methods
and details of his results in 13 volumes of his *Psychological Mono-*

graphs series. To have done this at all is a remarkable achievement and to have done it in two languages, with French and English texts on facing pages, is Herculean. The last two volumes alone have almost 400 pages each. How much of this is due to the redoubtable Francoise I cannot say, but they are a formidable team.

For the record, Series A (Vols. 1 to 6) gives the birth data and planetary distributions of Gauquelin's professional notabilities (over 16,000 with birth times): Series B (Vols. 1 to 6) gives the same for the 25,000 parents and children who formed the basis of the heredity experiment, and Series C, Vol. 1, gives the summary statistical results obtained from all the foregoing data. Thus has Gauquelin silenced empty criticism; disbelievers must either swallow his findings and shut up or get down to work and show where he went wrong: all the information is available to them.

But from Series C, Vol. 2, events take a different turn and although Gauquelin described, in part, the new work at our conference last year (1973) I think most listeners did not fully take in the scope and implications of this research.

The findings of the new series of investigations are more specifically and distinctively astrological than most of Gauquelin's earlier work—or at least they take a big step forward along that road—and they are best understood as complementary to the work which the present writer and others have done on harmonics in astrology.

In order to understand the remarkable experiments which Gauquelin has carried out and which are described in this article (those on the Mars temperament and sports champions and Saturn and scientists) we must cast our mind back to his earlier results.

Having compiled large collections of the nativities of various professional groups, he analyzed the distribution of each of the planets *in its diurnal circle* (i.e., house position) for each group separately.

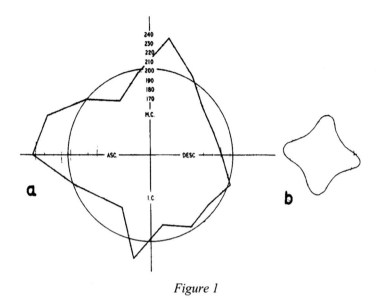

Figure 1

He found that with each group a distinctive pattern emerged for some or all of the planets and generally speaking it was found that the planets which conventional astrology would normally relate to particular professions (as: Mars for athletes, Saturn for scientists, etc.) occupied to an outstanding degree, the sectors of the diurnal circle which followed after their rising and upper culmination—in other words the twelfth and ninth houses. As a rule the strength of the sixth and third houses are less pronounced, nevertheless there was every indication that the distribution of such a planet through the houses was dominated by the fourth harmonic. Here is a typical example (figure 1a): it shows the distribution of Saturn in the diurnal circle in the nativities of 3,647 scientists and physicians. Figure 1b for comparison shows a wave form representing a 4th harmonic distribution. (Here, in 1a, Guaquelin is using 18 divisions instead of the 12 traditional in astrology.)

This kind of fourth harmonic figure tends to dominate the planetary distribution of Gauquelin's professional groups and I have frequently tried to indicate why this should be so. I believe the fourth harmonic is strongest in these cases because the number four is connected with the idea of work, of striving, of *effort and achievement* (we must remember that Gauquelin's professionals are all men who *reached the top of their professions*). Four is also connected with the idea of *manifestation*. This is simply another way of looking at the same thing: the fourth, or material, cause is that which provides resistance and so requires effort, and will-power if something is to be made a manifest reality . . . hence the "difficult" character of the square, but hence, too, the reason why squares[11] provide an opportunity for us to actualize the potentialities which would otherwise lie dormant for want of the actual circumstances in which, alone, they can be unfolded.

Now Gauquelin does not present his work in terms of harmonics as such, nor indeed does he think primarily in these terms; as a statistician he is content, at present, to demonstrate the high statistical significance of the ascertained distributions in order to make his point. Nevertheless it is with divisions of the circle by symbolic whole numbers that we are, in reality, dealing, and if we wish to bring order and meaning out of his results it is in these terms that we, as astrologers, must learn to think.

With this in mind I have again, tried elsewhere, to show that not all Gauquelin's results are equally dominated by the 4th harmonic and we can easily find examples of other symbolic numbers at work. Here, for example (figure 2a), is the distribution of Mars in the nativities of 2,088 sports champions.

Now it is fairly easy to see here that the dominant in fluence is the third harmonic (see figure 2b). Nevertheless we can also see that Gauquelin has his high-scoring areas in the twelfth and ninth houses, just as if he had a fourth harmonic going for him. What are we to make of that?

---

[11]Squares, and all other aspects which result from the division of the circle by a multiple of four (i.e. 8,12,16, 20, etc.).

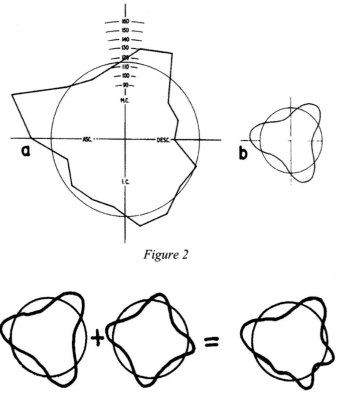

Figure 2

Figure 3

   The answer (which is quite visible to the naked eye, so to
speak, when one is used to looking at such things) becomes clear
when the distribution is subjected to an exact mathematical analysis: the distribution is predominantly determined by a combination
of the third and fourth harmonics in almost equal quantities, with
the third slightly the stronger. Phased as in figure 3, the two harmonics more or less reinforce each other in the region of the
twelfth and ninth houses but do not coincide so closely in the region of the fifth house and so produce there a more flattened
high-scoring plateau.

This gives us a chance to look at a full harmonic analysis and to see how it is expressed. For most readers this is something new yet it is easy to understand. Peter Smith has subjected a number of Gauquelin's diurnal distributions to harmonic analysis by computer, using the distribution totals by 36 sectors given in Series C, Vol. 1. Here is the analysis of the sports champions Mars distribution:

Harmonic	Amplitude	Phase	Harmonic	Amplitude	Phase
1	9.1	16	9	4.9	248
2	8.3	95	10	3.9	179
3	12.4	356	11	2.6	243
4	12.1	56	12	4.9	257
5	6.8	122	13	4.3	272
6	4.6	78	14	1.2	88
7	4.3	27	15	6.0	287
8	4.8	170	16	7.2	342
			17	5.1	294

Explanation of Table

Without attempting to explain why it is that with the distribution given by 36 totals the analysis can be taken to the 17th harmonic (half of 36, less one), we will note only that the first column gives the number of the harmonic, column two the amplitude of that harmonic and column three its phase.

The amplitude simply tells *how strong* each harmonic is, and we can see straight away that there are two harmonics of outstanding presence, namely the 3rd (12.4 percent) and the 4th (12.1 percent). (It is worth mentioning that in a later experiment, by comparing the maps of *very outstanding* athletes with those of ordinarily successful ones, Gauquelin demonstrated that the amplitude was higher in direct proportion to the degree of attainment.)

Column three tells us *whereabouts* in the circle the peaks

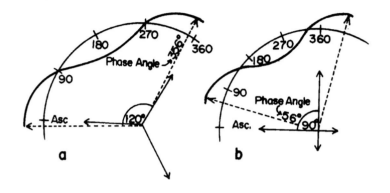

Figure 4

come and the way it is expressed is very simple. As we know the 3rd harmonic divides the circle into three, showing three waves of 120° each, the 4th divides it into four waves of 90° each. But for the purposes of the phase angle each wavelength is treated as if it were one complete circle or circle of 360° (no matter what its actual length is as a fraction of the *whole* circle) and the phase angle is the point along that 360° scale where the peak of the wave comes. *Measurements in the diurnal circle are from the Ascendant.*

Thus in figure 4a we can see that the first 120° of the diurnal circle is divided by a 360 scale and we can see that the third harmonic of Gauquelin's sports champions is phased at 356 along the scale (see table above) so that the peak almost coincides with the ninth cusp (and, therefore, of course, with the Ascendant and fifth cusp, too). In the second case (figure 4b) we have the first 90° of the circle divided by a 360° scale, and here the peak comes at 56° (see table).

We can now see clearly, if we look again at the three parts of figure 3, why Gauquelin has got his high scores in the twelfth and ninth houses—the two parts of the circle where the 3rd and 4th harmonics most closely coincide.

So far, so good. We now come to Gauquelin's experiments that take the matter fascinatingly a step further.

Although Gauquelin had established indisputably that the nativities of those in different professions showed *en masse*, so to speak, clear tendencies towards certain planetary positions, yet he had not sought to justify a direct link between these positions and any supposed character traits (or other tendencies) allegedly possessed by members of the professions in question. In order, therefore, to see if this could be done he chose the sports champions—possibly because they had yielded a strong result but also, no doubt, because they presented an easier problem in terms of character traits—and he asked three different sets of people: "What are the characteristics which distinguish the sports champion?"

First, he inquired what *psychologists* had written about the high-achievement athlete. Secondly, he considered the expressed opinions of *specialists in sport*—trainers, sportswriters, and athletes themselves. Thirdly, he contrived a questionnaire in which the *educated public* was asked for thoughts on what made a sports champion.

The result was interesting if perhaps predictable. All three groups gave the same answer: in a word, "guts." As if to emphasize that, both ancient and modern writers support this view. Gauquelin prefaces this section of his book with a quotation from Seneca: "The public admires the arms and legs of the athletes; I admire their courage." He quotes, among others, Dr. Roger Bannister: "In sport the training requires a will of iron, a hardness towards oneself of which few men are capable."

So, it being agreed that sheer willpower is what the sports champion has that the others have not, Gauquelin then compiled a list of words descriptive of the champions' character traits. In order to do this, he made use not only of the words used by the psychologists and others, but he also made use of a dictionary of synonyms employing the technique of a "center-word" with its derivative synonyms. Thus, using the word "WILL," a short-list of synonyms was yielded:

Character (to have), decided, energetic, firm, persistent, resolute.

These words, again, were looked up and gave a "second generation" of synonyms:

Strenuous, assurance, audacious, authority, constant, courageous, plucky, determined, dynamic, long-suffering, strong, bold, impassive, inflexible, male, obdurate, grip (has), resilient, coolness, tenacious, stubborn, vigorous.

And this list again when followed up further, gave a larger "third generation" of appropriate words, from:

Self-assured, ardent, assiduous . . . to . . . valorous, virile and vitality.

Thus (and I am necessarily simplifying the story a little) Gauquelin built up a list of 149 words which referred to the character of sports champions. He then went back to the works of reference giving brief biographies whence his original list of champions was drawn and reading carefully through the biographical notes of each champion the words which appeared in his list of 149 character traits were underlined whenever they were used to describe one of the champions. Thus it could say, of one man that ". . . he has *decided* opinions, is *tenacious* in pursuing his ambitions and assiduous in his training schedule . . ."

Notice that for each word underlined in the description of a particular athlete, *the position of Mars in that man's nativity counts once in the final tally.* If he has 10 willpower words then his Mars position counts 10 times, if he has three such words his Mars counts three times. In this way a Mars distribution pattern is derived which is specifically if approximately, related to the quality of willpower and its associated concepts.

We shall see what this distribution is shortly but first we must follow through to the next step in this experiment which is of crucial importance. In order to obtain, for contrast, a Mars distribution which correlates with the characteristics which are *opposite* to those of the typical champion, Gauquelin made a list of *antonyms* of his first list, this gives him two lists of almost equal length; the one (which we have already dealt with) beginning with: accrocheur (grasping), acharre (strenuous), actif (active), agite (restless) . . . and the other with: adaptable, adorable, affable, agreeable!

Gauquelin then went through his biographies again, underlining any words from the second list which were used to describe his sports champions. And again, for each such word used that man's Mars position went into a second pool which thus yielded another Mars distribution, this time specifically relating to the characteristics *opposite* to those of the alleged topical champion.

Needless to say, more positions (2,299) were obtained for the first set of words than for the second (1,109)—obviously since the biographies were distinctively those of men who allegedly possessed an abundance of the characteristics given in the first list. Nevertheless, enough of the athletes were "adaptable," "agreeable," etc. (some were even described as "gentlemen"—a fatal attribute in the would-be champion) to allow the second contrasting set of Mars positions to be extracted.

This was a daring and ingenious ploy because, as the reader will have noticed, the emphasis of the study is now no longer on sports champions as such (for both sets of positions are those of sports champions) but on Mars positions as correlated with two sets of character traits, the first assertive and uncompromising, the second yielding and moderate. Notice that if one of the champions is described as "audacious," "strong," "impassive," and "energetic" then his Mars position goes into the first count four times, but if he is also described as "adaptable" and "courteous," then it also goes into the second count twice. Only someone with a real

176

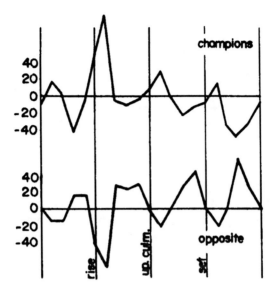

Figure 5

grasp of the potentialities of the statistical method will devise tactics of this kind.

What then did these two sets of Mars positions show? Remember that we are dealing with the position of Mars in its diurnal circle, divided into 18 sectors. The answer is shown in figure 5. Here the top line shows the distribution pattern of Mars (above or below the expected frequency) in those with the characteristics of the typical sports champion; the bottom line shows the distribution for those with the opposite characteristics.

This is a remarkable result for it will be seen that the two patterns are a mirror-image of each other; where one is high the other is low and vice versa. (The vertical scale is more elongated in the second line because there were only half as many cases of the "yielding" qualities.)

This diagram will repay careful study and thought on the part of those who are interested in extending our understanding of psychological qualities in relation to astrology. It asks many questions as well as answering some but in general terms it indicates that when the Mars principle is examined in relation to the faculty of WILL it shows a fourth harmonic distribution with positive phases reaching their highest intensity some 15° to 20° after the angles, and this is confirmed by the second graph which shows the opposite (yielding, moderate) qualities to be at their minimum strength when Mars is in these positions.

But it shows something else which is very arresting. If we look back at figure 2a and at the table of harmonic analysis we can see that in the *original* study of sports champions, before any attempt was made to link up with character traits, the distribution of Mars was dominated by the third and fourth harmonics with the third slightly the stronger. *Now*, if we looked at figure 5 we can see that the third harmonic has virtually vanished and that the distribution is quite clearly a fourth harmonic pattern—four peaks, four troughs. What happened to the third harmonic?

With this in mind I was not surprised to have a note from Professor Gauquelin acknowledging the copies which we sent him of Peter Smith's harmonic analyses of his results: ". . . thank you so much for the documents about harmonic analysis . . . for me the most intriguing result you have is about sports champions (Mars). Here you find a third harmonic; but this result is not consistent with our last results published in Volume II, Series C, with the personality traits. How do you explain the difference?"

I was able to reply by return. I explained that in my view the reason for the change in the result when the emphasis was switched from the *sports champions themselves* to a list of *their alleged characteristics* was quite simply that the character of the sports champion had been *misjudged* and that all the experts, in ascribing the dominant character traits had partly missed the point: "I don't think there can be much doubt about what has happened. The experts have laid by far the greater emphasis on sheer hard *will-*

power and not enough on zest, enjoyment, creativity, inspiration and even "showmanship." I was very struck by this when I saw the results of your personality analysis.

"I have therefore made a list of synonyms which I think provide the third harmonic factor. Some of them overlap with your "hard" synonyms, some with your "soft" synonyms, but basically they represent a different idea. It is a question of the "heart" rather than the "will." The key words are:

(1) Enjoyment, appetite, zest, gusto

(2) Creativity

(3) Inspiration, and the ability to inspire and animate others, including leadership (which involves claiming the loyalty and affection of others)

(4) Possibly an element of showmanship. (Not a necessary element of the true champion but frequently present as an underlying factor.)

"I suspect that all these would tend to be third harmonic elements."

I enclosed a list of 100 words compiled with the help of *Roget's Thesaurus* and expressed the hope that at least a pilot study would be made, using this list or a similar one, to see if, in this way, the fourth harmonic could be filtered out and the third harmonic left standing, just as before the third had been filtered out and the fourth left.

Professor Gauquelin has agreed that he will tackle this in due course and it will be extremely interesting to see what emerges. I am not sure that I have identified the third harmonic factors and those only, but most students will probably agree that I am on the right lines.

Before ending this assessment of the sports champions' character trait study it should be said that it is *not only the Mars positions* which show an opposite (mirror image) distribution pattern between the two contrasting character groups, but also Moon, Venus, Jupiter and Saturn, but in those cases the contrast is less powerful. Nevertheless it is fairly clear and will no doubt contribute valuable evidence when the time comes for a synthesis of these findings.

In Part II of this article we will look (more briefly!) at the Saturn temperament and scientists.

Chapter 14

Michel Gauquelin Strikes Again, Part II

In Part I of this article I described an experiment carried out by Michel and Francoise Gauquelin in which they attempted to relate the planetary positions in the nativities of sports champions (especially of Mars) to actual character traits.

I explained how they made a list of "willpower" words ("tough," "resolute," etc.), then went through the biographies of sports champions and for each time that one of these was used for a particular champion, his Mars position counted once.

Having then, for contrast, compiled a list of character traits *opposite* to those of the typical champion, the same biographies of champions were scrutinized for these words and for each such "non-champion" character trait attributed to a particular sportsman, *his* Mars position counted once in a second tally of Mars positions.

It was shown that the distributions of Mars in the diurnal circle for these two sets of nativities were exactly opposite (see figure 5 in Part I), that the parts of the diurnal circle occupied by Mars when related to the hard, tough, aggressive character traits were the parts which were *not* occupied by Mars when related to the gentler, more moderate characteristics and vice versa.

I also pointed out that whereas in Gauquelin's complete list of sports champions, when studied without any regard to their alleged characteristics, the Mars distribution was dominated by the 3rd harmonic (with the 4th harmonic second in strength), yet when the will-power characteristics were introduced and made the basis of the Mars distribution, the 3rd harmonic was, in effect, filtered out and the 4th harmonic left standing.

I suggested that this was because the characteristics of the sports champion had been falsely assessed as being all "guts" and aggression and that the capacity for zest, enthusiasm and enjoyment had not been given due weight. It remains to be seen if, by studying the same group of sporting nativities in relation to the supposed 3rd harmonic characteristics of zest and enthusiasm, the 4th harmonic can be filtered out and the 3rd left standing.

In Volume 3 of the Series C of their *Psychological Monographs* the Gauquelins tackle the Saturn temperament and scientists.

They employ the same sort of tactics as in their study of sports champions. First they enquire what the characteristics of the typical scientists are supposed to be, examining studies of the psychology of scientists already made and putting a questionnaire to members of the educated public.

A number of studies have been made by psychologists of the typical scientist's temperament. Here, for example, is the list of words given by Anne Roe (1966: Independent Research Scientists, all fields):

> "adapted, well adjusted, anguished, anxious, calm, academic, concrete, continuity, good control, conventional, headstrong, distaste for the imaginary, unquiet, unsociable, not mundane, objective, obstinate, persistent, not original, placid, reassured, rational, realistic, rebellious, refractory, takes responsi-

bilities, restive, serene, retarded psycho-sexually, tenacious, stubborn, tranquil."

Other lists bring out other characteristics and it should be said, I think, that some of these lists evidently suffer from having been translated from English into French and then back again by different hands with the result that some of the niceties have been lost. For example, one of the qualities attributed to the scientists (and which scores quite heavily) is that they are "soft." The French word here is "doux" and I take it that the quality observed is that they tend to be *gentle* (*not* self-indulgent and flabby which is what we understand by "soft"). However, the overall picture arrived at is clear and would probably be accepted as, in general, a good description of the typical scientist's temperament.

Proceeding as before, the Gauquelins first extend their list of character trait words, using a dictionary of synonyms, then they read through the biographical dictionaries describing the individual scientists and for each time one of the list of their (250) character words is used for a particular scientist, the Saturn position of that scientist counts once. In this way 3,209 Saturn positions were recorded.

Next a list of antonyms of the above words was made—descriptive of the characteristics *opposite* to those of the typical scientist. Again the biographical notes on each scientist were examined and for each time that one of the second list of words was used of a particular scientist, that person's Saturn position counted once. In this way a second pool of 2,554 Saturn positions was acquired, these being specifically related to the characteristics opposite to those of the typical scientist.

Now before looking at these two sets of Saturn positions let us again look at the Saturn distribution for *all* scientists (3,647 in number) before they were studied in relation to character traits. This was given in Part 1 of this article (figure 1a) in the form of a circular graph. Here it is again—figure 6—in a more straight-for-

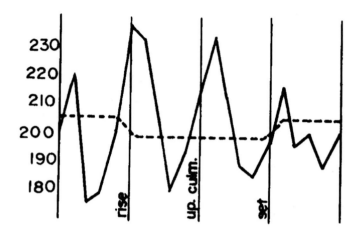

Figure 6

ward form, and we can see quite clearly that by far the strongest and dominant element is a 4th harmonic; four peaks and four troughs spaced out at 90° intervals just at or after the rising, setting and upper and lower culminations. The peaks are not of equal strength but there is no doubt at all that it is a 4th harmonic distribution.

Let us now look at the two sets of Saturn positions based upon the study of character traits; these are shown in figure 7. The top line here shows the distribution of Saturn in relation to the typical personality of the scientist. The bottom line shows Saturn's position when correlated with the characteristics *opposite* to the typical scientist's.

There are two striking features. First we can see again that the distribution patterns are exactly opposite each other, the one being high where the other is low, showing quite clearly that the opposite character-traits do correlate with an opposite diurnal distribution.

But just as striking is the fact that the original dominant 4th harmonic has been filtered out and replaced by a 5th harmonic!

184

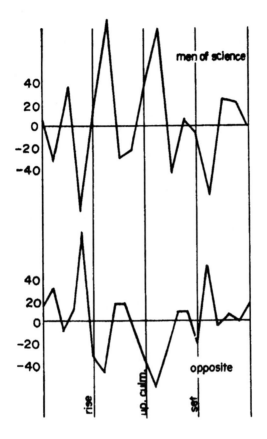

Figure 7

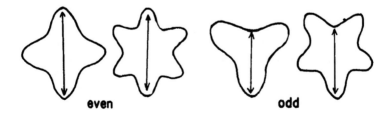

Figure 8

This again *is not in the least in doubt.* The five peaks are quite evenly spaced round the circle and whereas the 4th harmonic (being even-numbered) the peaks in the twelfth and ninth houses are opposed by peaks in the sixth and third houses, in this graph, showing a dominant 5th harmonic, the peaks in the twelfth and ninth are opposed by *troughs* in the sixth and third. (All even-numbered harmonics have peaks opposite peaks, all odd-numbered harmonics have peaks opposite troughs.)

What is the explanation of this? My own view is quite simply that again the dominant characteristics of the typical successful[12] scientist have been misjudged. A careful reading of Gauquelin's full list of words descriptive of the scientists' temperament shows that they are very strongly weighted with mental characteristics. Anne Roe's list given above is not entirely typical in this respect but the full list shows a very strong tendency to emphasize mental character traits, not surprisingly.

I have again suggested to M. Gauguelin that he should follow this up and that by applying the willpower to his biographies of successful scientists (ambitious, determined, uncompromising, etc.) he should be able to filter out the 5th harmonic shown so clearly in this result and restore the 4th harmonic which was originally so strong.

These two experiments (one with the sports champions, one with the scientists) which I have suggested would, if successful, give us an interesting set of basic correlations:

- Three = the heart (enjoyment, enthusiasm)
- Four = the will (difficulty-effort-achievement)
- Five = the mind (discrimination, analysis, thoughtfulness)

It will be of interest to show another example of the planetary distributions derived by Gauquelin from his comparison of the scientist's temperament and its opposite.

---

[12] Successful, that is, in the worldly sense.

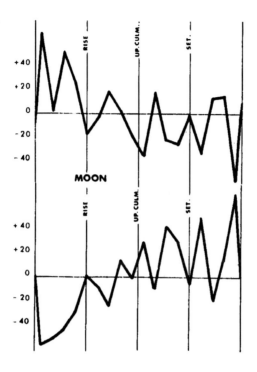

Figure 9

Figure 9 shows the distribution of the Moon in the diurnal circle for the scientific temperament (top line) and opposite temperament. The striking feature here being the peak in the third house for scientific temperament, and a deep trough in the third house for the non-scientific type. We can again see that the combination of harmonics for the two types is exactly opposite but that the precise combination is not a simple matter of one dominant harmonic but of two or three different harmonics working together.

Incidentally this is a very good example of one of the classical harmonic combinations; it is the one in which the ascending nodes of the waves, or the descending nodes in the case of the temperament opposite to the scientists', all coincide at one point in the cir-

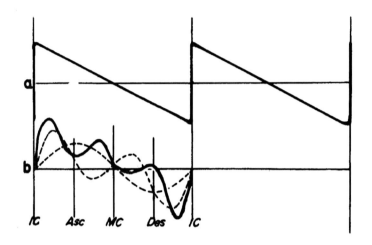

Figure 10

cle—in this case at the IC. If developed this gives a saw-toothed effect (figure 10a) which is arrived at as shown in 10b: all waves starting to rise at one point. If more and more harmonics are added on this basis the saw teeth become more and more pointed.

The last of the studies to be published: *The Jupiter Temperament and Actors* does not present any anomaly of the kind we have described in relation to sports champions or scientists. Jupiter shows a very strong 4th in all actors taken together and a strong 4th when the same maps are examined by character trait. This is the "will" aspect of Jupiter—a lot of extroverts all trying to fight their way into the footlights glare.

Chapter 15

Sex of Offspring and Father's Moon Position

In *American Astrology* for February 1971, the late Donald A. Bradley, writing under the name of Garth Allen, reported somewhat briefly of a study he had made of the Moon position (in the zodiac) of fathers, in relation to the sex of their children.

The data studied consisted of the birth dates of 654 men with two or more sons and no daughters and 546 men with two or more daughters and no sons.

Bradley found that the ratio of "boyers" to "girlers" (Bradley's designation of the fathers of male and female progeny respectively) showed a distinct variation of natal Moon position in each 90° of the zodiac such that there was a high proportion of "boyers" with the Moon in the fixed signs (Taurus, Leo, Scorpio, Aquarius) and a predominance of "girlers" with the Moon in the common, or mutable, signs (Gemini, Virgo, Sagittarius and Pisces).

Figure 1 shows, against the scale of probabilities, the ratio of boy-fathers to girl-fathers according to the Moon's position in the quadruplicities—that is to say on a 4th harmonic basis. A 30° moving total of Moon positions was used by Bradley for this comparison, a technique which is, as we have observed before, useful for showing some things and a nuisance in the way it conceals others.

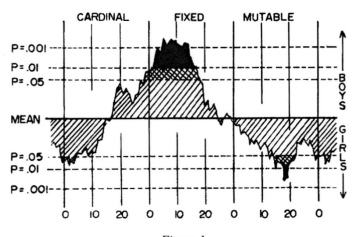

Figure 1
30° Moving Totals in Tropical Longitude

Bradley gave no further details in the form of precise totals, nor did he give the source of his data (though it should be said that, due to the prejudices against astrology, the researcher in this field is sometimes placed in a position in which he cannot reveal his source).

In order to provide some sort of check on these findings the Astrological Association Research Section made use of two sources of information giving appropriate data.

1. In the large collection of family birth data made by Michel Gauquelin and used by him for his inquiry into the link between astrological factors and hereditary ones, Gauquelin gives some 25,000 birth dates (with approximate times of birth) of parents and children collected from birth registers in France. In many of these families the fathers' data is not given; in many more there is only one child or the family is of mixed sexes. However, in all cases where the fathers' data was given and where the family consisted of two or more boys only, or two or more girls only, the father's Moon position was duly calculated.

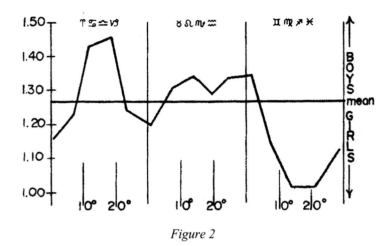

Figure 2

In addition, and in order to swell the totals, we included in the study all those cases where the family had boys or girls in the ratio of at least three of one sex to one of the other. All this yielded 272 boy-fathers and 216 girl-fathers, a total of 488 Moon positions.

All this rather large operation was tackled singlehanded by Christel Garrick of the Astrological Association to whom due acknowledgment is made.

There is one point which should be mentioned in passing. It would seem that the method adopted by Gauquelin in extracting his birth data from local registers did not preclude the situation where the parents may have moved away from the district where Gauquelin's births were registered *and then had children of a different sex elsewhere*. Similarly they may have had children *before* moving to that district. However, it can be safely assumed that the two sets of fathers' birth data *are* very heavily based towards boyers or girlers.

It seemed adequate in this first attempt to reproduce Bradley's results to give the ratio of boyers to girlers at six-degree intervals and figure 2 therefore shows the ratio of boy-fathers to girl-fathers in the 4th harmonic based on 30° moving totals at intervals of 6°.

Here we see that the ratio of boyers to girlers is again low in the common or mutable Signs, as with Bradley's results. But we also see that the highest ratio of boyers to girlers falls somewhat earlier in the 90° sectors, that is in the later part of the cardinal signs rather than at the beginning of the fixed signs. However, the overall picture is not entirely dissimilar from Bradley's result and, indeed, gives some support to it.

2. A second attempt was made to verify Bradley's findings using *Who Was Who 1951-60*. Peggy Lance extracted from this reference work all those men whose date of birth was listed and who had two or more sons and no daughters or vice versa. This yielded 499 girl-fathers and 451 boy-fathers.

The Moon's position at noon for these men was tabulated and examined in precisely the same way as Bradley's original sample. Thus figure 3, which shows this result, plots the ratio of fathers of sons to fathers of daughters according to Moon position in cardinal, fixed and mutable signs. Again, a 30° moving total has been used so that each point on the graph represents the ratio between totals of Moon positions for 15° on either side of that position.

It can be seen that there is again a strong preponderance of boyers with the Moon in cardinal signs, as with the Gauquelin data and that, in fact, all three graphs (Bradley, Gauquelin, Who Was Who) show a distinct resemblance, indicating in broad terms that when the Moon in a man's horoscope occupies the first half of the quadruplicities, i.e., from 0° cardinals to 15° fixed, there is a tendency to produce male offspring, and when it falls between 15° fixed, and the end of the mutables, there is a tendency to produce female offspring.

The results are at least sufficiently striking to warrant a much fuller study of this subject.

192

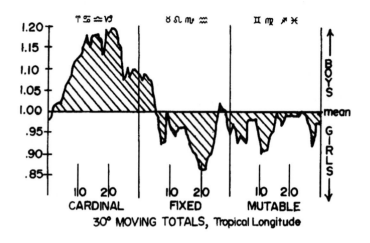

Figure 3

It should be noted that although we have been content to show, in this account, the tendency to a 4th harmonic correspondence between results, nevertheless there were a number of features of the Astrological Association's two experiments which seemed to suggest the significant involvement of other harmonic elements in the Moon's positions.

For example it was found that the three lowest sign totals for three or more girls were:

- *Who Was Who*: 1. Aquarius, 2. Aries, 3. Gemini and 4. Cancer
- Gauquelin data: 1. Cancer, 2. Aries, 3. Aquarius
- The four highest sign-totals for three or more girls were:
- *Who Was Who*: 1. Leo, 2. Sagittarius, 3. Scorpio Pisces, 4. Taurus.
- Gauquelin: 1. Scorpio, 2. Sagittarius, 3. Virgo Pisces, 4. Taurus.

For the boys, Moon in Aquarius was highest in both studies.

A limited study of other harmonics in the *Who Was Who* data showed the 9th to be even stronger than the 4th.

One comment which might be made upon the difference in phasing of the 4th harmonic in the three sets of data which, it will be noted, came from three different countries, is that in the many studies of periodic phenomena made by the Foundation for the Study of Cycles, of Pittsburgh, just such variations are often to be found in the peak timing of cycles at different places on Earth's surface and this variation is evidently found to be associated with magnetic declination.

CPSIA information can be obtained
at www.ICGtesting.com
Printed in the USA
FSOW01n1248090816
23411FS